T0078005

Invocations Inspired by the Qur'an

Hanif D. Sherali

authorHOUSE®

AuthorHouse™
1663 Liberty Drive
Bloomington, IN 47403
www.authorhouse.com
Phone: 1 (800) 839-8640

Published by AuthorHouse 06/30/2020

ISBN: 978-1-7283-6582-4 (sc)
ISBN: 978-1-7283-6583-1 (hc)
ISBN: 978-1-7283-6600-5 (e)

Library of Congress Control Number: 2020911670

Dedicated to my parents and
to the memory of my son, Azeem

June, 2020

Preface

Aozobillahi Minash Shaitaan Nir-rajeem.
Bismillah Hir-Rahmaan Nir-Raheem.
I seek refuge in Allah from the accursed devil.
In the Name of Allah, the Beneficent, the Merciful.

Allah (SWT)* asks us to seek refuge in Him from the accursed devil whenever we recite the Glorious Qur'an (16:98) [1, 2], and also asks us to repel evil with what is best and to say, "My Lord, I seek refuge in Thee from the evil suggestions of the devils, and I seek refuge in Thee, my Lord, lest they come to me" (23:96-98). Furthermore, whenever we begin reciting the Qur'an, or for that matter, commence any task, we do so by declaring that it is in the Name of Allah, the Beneficent, the Merciful (*Bismillah Hir-Rahmaan Nir-Raheem*). The Messenger of Allah (SAW)* said that any task that is initiated with *Bismillah Hir-Rahmaan Nir-Raheem* is blessed, and otherwise, it is doomed from the very start.

Curiously, in the English language, the word "Devil" begins with the letter "D", and there exist a slew of "d"isliked items that all start with the letter "d", similar to the stated name of *Shaitaan* – Devil: distress, discord, dissent, disputes, danger, disasters, discrimination, damage, depravity, disdain, dismay, deluge, delusions, debt, destruction, desolation, divisiveness, disappointment, discouragement, dejection, deceit, defeat, dependence, disgrace, despair, desperation, disrespect, decrepitude, dementia, defamation, diseases, depression, degradation, dictatorships, dishonesty, dissonance, distrust, disbelief in Allah (SWT) - may Allah (SWT) protect us from all of these as well as from the evil inclinations of the deplorable, demonic Devil.

Likewise, similar to the starting letter "B" in *Bismillah*, the blessed beginning of it all, we ask Allah (SWT) to grant us Blessings and Barakah in all our affairs, Beauty in our souls, Beneficence from Him with Benefit to all, by His Grace and Mercy, Bliss in our minds and hearts, Big-heartedness in our acts of charity, Bravery in all our initiatives, Brightness and Brilliance in our thoughts, words, and actions, Balance in our approach to all endeavors, and the Best of rewards from the Almighty Lord for the Best of our deeds in the life of this world as well as in the Hereafter, Ameen.

This book is comprised of invocations or supplications (*du'aa*) that are inspired by various sets of selected stimulating verses from the Qur'an, which, in themselves, are particularly worthy of pondering and reflecting upon. The fundamental concept here is that, while reading the Qur'an, if one recites a verse that elicits a certain thought or emotion, then one should make a corresponding invocation in its reflection. It was the practice of Prophet Muhammad (SAW) when reciting the Qur'an that when he would come to a verse glorifying Allah (SWT) he would glorify Him, when he would recite a verse of forgiveness or mercy or favor or blessing from Allah (SWT), he would request it of Him, and when he would recite a verse describing punishment from Allah (SWT), he would seek refuge in his Lord from chastisement and implore Him for well-being [7]. Accordingly, while reading the Qur'an, when Allah (SWT) mentions some characteristic that is pleasing to Him, the reader should make a supplication to His Lord to instill that characteristic within him or her. Likewise, when we recite a verse where Allah (SWT) disdains an action or behavioral characteristic, we should invoke Him to guide us and assist us in avoiding such a pitfall. It is in this spirit that the present book is composed.

As such, this book is not intended to collect specific verses from the Qur'an that *directly* comprise du'aas, which are popularly described in many publications, although such powerful verses do indeed prompt du'aas in the present work as well. For example, in Surah

Baqarah (2:201), Allah (SWT) prescribes a beautiful comprehensive du'aa for Muslims, which was most frequently invoked by the Prophet (SAW) as narrated in Sahih Al-Bukhari (Ch. 75:57), *"Rabbana Aatina Fid-Dunya Hasanatau; Wa Fil Aakhirati Hasanatau; Wa Qina Adhaab-an-Naar"* - Our Lord, grant us good in this world; and good in the Hereafter; and save us from the chastisement of the Fire. Several such supplications are prescribed in the Qur'an, many of which have been made by different prophets under different circumstances, which afford powerful invocations under parallel situations, preferably in the original Arabic text as revealed by Allah (SWT). The invocations composed in this book are not just based on such directly supplicating verses, but also on various inspirational collection of verses from the Qur'an that move one's heart and prompt a heartfelt supplication in response. The reader is encouraged to revisit and ponder and reflect on these verses. Furthermore, the style of the invocations is in the framework of a discourse, inviting the readers to join in the plea. These invocations can also be made in a first-person direct conversation with the Almighty Lord, the Most High.

Allah (SWT) says in Surah *Al –Mu'min* (40:60), "And your Lord says: Call on Me (pray to Me), I will answer you." May Allah (SWT) inspire in us invocations that are consonant with His Grand Plan and Purpose for our creation as per His Pleasure, so that we are well-pleased, Ameen.

Hanif D. Sherali
June, 2020

---

* See *Glossary of Terms* at the end of the book for abbreviations and definitions.

We ask Allah (SWT), the Most Compassionate and Merciful Lord of the universe to Whom all praise is due exclusively, and the Master Who is in complete control at all times, a clear manifestation of which will occur on the Day of Judgement, to grant us the most precious gift of guidance to the right path that leads to His Pleasure, worshiping Him alone and serving all of mankind with goodness in the process, and we beseech Him for His help and support in this endeavor so that we are among the most fortunate ones – the prophets, the truthful, the faithful, and the righteous - on whom He has bestowed His treasured favors, not among those who have earned His wrath nor those who have gone astray; and we entreat Him to forgive us and have mercy on us, for this is surely our all-encompassing need, and He is indeed the Most Forgiving, Most Merciful, Ameen (*as inspired by the Qur'an, 1:1-7, the seven oft-repeated verses (15:87), which are a source of light for all of mankind.*)

We ask Allah (SWT) to grant us His most precious gift of guidance, as revealed in the Glorious Qur'an and through the teaching and practice of His beloved Prophet (SAW), and to make us among His close ones who are God-conscious and who keep their duty towards Him and guard against evil, and who believe in the unseen with surety of heart and faith, and who uphold the two main tenets of Islam by worshipping Him, and Him alone, devotedly, and serve Him by performing acts of goodness and charity toward all with kindness of heart, for surely, such are the ones whom He has set on a right course and who are successful in the life of this world as well as in the Hereafter, and upon whom there shall alight no fear, nor shall they grieve; and we beseech Him to separate us from the ones who are heedless of His guidance and warnings, and who break His covenants and cut asunder what He has commanded to be joined, and who lie and make mischief in the land, even while proclaiming themselves to be peacemakers, and in whose hearts is a disease so that their Lord has intensified this disease, for such are the unfortunate losers who will be paid back their mockery by their Lord, and whose hearts and hearing have been sealed and whose eyes have been covered by Him, so that they are spiritually deaf, dumb, and blind, left blindly wandering in their inordinacy; and we entreat the Almighty Lord to make us among His righteous servants who submit to Him and who worship and serve Him and perform overarching acts of goodness, so that we receive the good news in the Hereafter, in reflection of our deeds in this life, of pure companions in magnificent Gardens wherein rivers flow, which, as our beloved Prophet (SAW) described, *no eye has seen and no ear has heard, nor has it entered into the heart of man to conceive of them*, all by the Grace and Mercy of our Lord, the Most High, for surely, He is oft returning to mercy, the Most Forgiving, Most Merciful, Ameen (*as inspired by the Qur'an, 2:2-7, 10-11, 15, 18, 21, 25, 27, 37-38*).

May Allah (SWT) guide us, and instill in us the fear of Him and Him alone, and may He inspire us to keep our duty foremost to Him and thereby toward all responsibilities we carry; and may He purify our hearts and minds so that we do not adulterate the truth with falsehood; and may He enable us to keep up prayer and be charitable toward all His creations; and may He enlighten us so that we prostrate ourselves with reverence along with His favored ones who bow down to Him and Him alone, and we enjoin goodness while not neglecting it for our own souls, and we seek His assistance exclusively through patience and prayer with humility, for this is indeed arduous except for the humble ones who recognize the purpose of their creation and know that they will meet their Lord and to Him they will return, Ameen (*as inspired by the Qur'an 2:40-46*).

4

May Allah (SWT), in Whose Hands is the Kingdom of the heavens and the earth, be our Protecting Friend and Helper, for besides Him there is no one who can be our protector or aid; and may He enable us to maintain a regimen of devoted worship of Him along with acts of kindness and charity, for whatever good we send beforehand in the life of this world, we shall indeed find it with Him in a purified and embellished form in the Hereafter by His Will; and may He guide us to submit wholly to Him, and Him alone, and to be among the doers of good to all, so that He rewards us amply for it, by His Grace and Mercy, and makes us among His chosen ones on whom there shall be no fear nor shall they grieve, Ameen (*as inspired by the Qur'an 2: 107, 110, 112*).

5

May Allah (SWT) grant us peace and contentment and bless us with the greatest and most noble of character-related gifts: *Sabr* – patience, forbearance, perseverance, tolerance, restraint, and resolve; and may He enhance our capacity of *Sabr* within our being and elevate the spirit of our acts of worship and our willingness to accept what He has decreed for us with grace, for *Sabr* is indeed a matter of immense resolution in the Eyes of Allah (SWT) for which He has promised a reward without any measure from His unlimited bounties; and may He inspire us to always be with Him and to seek His assistance through prayers and *Sabr,* for He is always with the patient ones who remain steadfast on the right course and who realize upon facing any trial or tribulation that they have after all come from Him, as has everything around and about them, and that they shall eventually return to Him with what their hands have sent forth, so that then there shall descend on them blessings and mercy from their Lord, the Most High, Who is the Beneficent and Merciful One, and the Lord of Mighty Grace toward all the worlds, and besides Whom there is no one or nothing worthy of worship, Ameen (*as inspired by the Qur'an, 2:153, 155-157, 163, 249-251; 39:10, 42:43*).

6

May Allah (SWT) enhance our awareness of Him; and may He enable us to perform our acts of devotion and service to Him with due reverence and sincerity, and to praise and laud Him in a manner that He alone deserves to be exalted, and to thank Him immensely for having guided us; and may He help us retain our focus on the eternity of the Hereafter while we implore Him for goodness in this life and in the afterlife; and may He make us among those who are always mindful of Him and who strive to sell themselves to seek His pleasure and who are in a state of complete peace and bliss, and who beg His forgiveness whenever they slip due to human weakness; and may He inspire us to feel His close presence to us and to hear His call and believe wholeheartedly in Him, so that we may walk along the right path, for indeed He answers the prayers of the supplicant servant who calls on Him fervently and with sincerity, and He is most compassionate to His servants, Ameen (*as inspired by the Qur'an, 2:185-186, 200-201, 207-208*).

May Allah (SWT), the Ever-Living and Self-subsisting One, the Most High and Great, illuminate and purify and enhance all our acts of *Ibadah*, and may He open our hearts to share generously the gifts He has blessed us with, for indeed everything in the heavens and the earth belongs to Him alone; and may He enable us to be ever aware of the day that is to come when there will be no bargaining, nor friendship, nor intercession except as He pleases, and may He grant us the favorable intercession of our beloved prophet Muhammad (SAW) on this day; and may He guide us to absorb and knit the Qur'an and the teachings of the Prophet (SAW) in our lives and thereby grasp the firmest possible handhold of support that shall never break; and may He be our Protecting Friend Who embraces us, and Who brings us into and preserves us in His Brilliant Light; and may He protect us from the evil machinations of the *Shaitaan* and his companions, and from them ever dragging us away into moral and spiritual darkness, all by His immense Grace and Mercy, Ameen (*as inspired by the Qur'an, 2:254-257*).

May Allah (SWT), the Owner of the Kingdom and the Master of the universe in Whose Hand is all goodness and control, gift us graciously of His Kingdom; and may he exalt us with honor and protect us from abasement; and may He bring us into light and illuminate our hearts just as the night passes into the day, and may He prevent us from ever elapsing into darkness; and may He gift us with spiritual life and brilliance through a perpetual remembrance of His Majesty, and may He prevent our souls from spiritual death and our hearts from hardening out of negligence of submission and service to Him; and may He grant us sustenance in this life and in the Hereafter without measure by His pleasure, for surely He has Power over all things; and may He never let our hearts deviate from this Guidance once conferred upon us by His Grace and Mercy, for indeed He is the most liberal and generous Giver and the gracious Preserver of Faith, Ameen (*as inspired by the Qur'an, 3:7, 25-26*).

9

May Allah (SWT) grant us guidance from Himself, for true guidance comes only from Him, and may He make our affairs and case prevail over the arguments and impediments of those whom He has chosen not to guide, and we pray that may we all love and obey Allah (SWT) and His beloved Prophet Muhammad (SAW) so that our Most Endearing, Benevolent, and Loving Creator loves us and grants us protection from the accursed devil along with forgiveness for our shortcomings and sins, and may He induce us to be devoted to His service and to worship Him alone and to remember and glorify Him day and night, so that He purifies our souls with beauty and goodness and grants us physical and spiritual sustenance abundantly by His Grace, for surely Grace is in His Hands alone and He gives it graciously to whomsoever He pleases without measure, being Ample-giving and All-knowing, and may He specially choose us among those whom He pleases to shower His immense Mercy, for He is indeed Most Merciful, and the Lord of Mighty Grace, Ameen (*as inspired by the Qur'an, 3:30-40, 72-73*).

10

May Allah (SWT) make our faces shine with glorious whiteness by His Grace and Mercy on the day when some faces will radiate with whiteness and others will be gloomy with blackness, and may He protect us from wrongdoing that might darken our faces, and may He reflect His Glory on our faces through the sight of His Countenance; and may He strengthen our hearts and souls with *Imaan* and *Taqwa* and Trust in Him; and may He remove any weakness in our hearts and souls and bodies and make us resolute and steadfast in His Path; and may the Almighty Lord grant us protection from any sins and evil inclinations and extravagance in our affairs; and may He establish us and firmly plant our feet and shape our desires along His Way according to His Will; and may He grant us victory and superiority over the arrogant disbelievers who are ungrateful and disobedient to Him; and may He make us among the doers of good whom He loves, so that we then earn a most gracious reward from Him in this world and in the Hereafter, and may He thereby admit us to the abode of perpetual peace in *Jannat-ul-Firdaus*, by His Grace and Mercy, Ameen (*as inspired by the Qur'an, 3:105-106, 145-147*).

11

May Allah (SWT) strengthen our hearts and defenses against those who strive against us and who try to instill fear of themselves within us, and may He render their attempts futile and make them only serve to instead increase our *Imaan* and to recognize that Allah (SWT) is altogether sufficient for us and is indeed an excellent Guardian, and that it is the *Shaitaan* who, ironically, frightens only his own friends regarding people and events, whereas the true believers fear Allah (SWT) and Him alone, so that then no evil touches us and we follow the pleasure of our Beloved Lord and Creator, and thereby return with favor from Him along with His Grace, for He is truly the Lord of Mighty Grace, Ameen (*as inspired by the Qur'an, 3:172-174*).

12

We pray to Allah (SWT) to enhance our understanding of His phenomenal and glorious creation of the heavens and the earth, and we ask Him to enable us to constantly abide in His remembrance, standing and sitting and lying on our sides, and to know with conviction that nothing and no one has been created in vain without purpose, and to open our hearts in the declaration that we have heard our beloved Prophet (SAW) calling us to the beautiful faith revealed to him by The Almighty Lord, and we have obeyed, hoping for forgiveness and mercy and purification, as well as for protection from evil inclinations and disgrace, as promised to the righteous doers of good by our Majestic Creator Himself, Who most assuredly never retracts from fulfilling His part of the promise, Ameen (*as inspired by the Qur'an, 3:189-193*).

13

May Allah (SWT) instill in us the intense desire and understanding to love and obey Him and His beloved Prophet Muhammad (SAW), and may He grant us His greatest gift of guidance and *Imaan* of the highest level so that we adopt His teachings, which He has revealed through the Wisdom of the Qur'an and the Sunnah of the Prophet (SAW), as our illuminated path in all our affairs, actions and judgments, with complete obedience and submission, never turning away from Him and finding no straitness in our hearts or the slightest inclination toward anything else; and may He protect us from any harm, temptation, and misguidance, none of which we can avert were it not for His benevolent Grace upon us and His Mercy; and may He beautify our speech as well as our secret counsels so that we enjoin what is good and charitable, and we encourage love and reconciliation between people while seeking His pleasure alone, and thereby earn from the All-Knowing One the greatest of rewards and favors of being placed among His choicest creations: the prophets, the truthful, the faithful, and the righteous, for such are the ones for whom He has reserved a mighty reward from Himself, and such is the Grace and Mercy of Allah (SWT), the Most Gracious, Most Merciful, Ameen (*as inspired by the Qur'an, 4:65, 67-70, 113-115*).

14

May Allah (SWT) illuminate our path and way of life with the light and guidance revealed by Him through the Glorious Qur'an, which is the illustrious *Muhaimin* (Guardian) and verifier in truth over all previous revelations, as well as through the enlightened Sunnah of our beloved Prophet Muhammad (SAW), so that we judge by these revelations and deviate not from the truth by following instead our own low desires, and that we vie with one another in performing virtuous deeds that are pleasing to our Creator; and we implore Him for ease and noble success in facing the trials and tests He places before us in order to draw us closer to Himself, for indeed, to Him is our eventual return when He, the Most Wise and Knowing One, will inform us of our acts and our innermost secrets, and as such, we find relief in knowing that, by His Benevolence, He is also the Most Forgiving, Merciful, Ameen (*as inspired by the Qur'an, 5:44, 46, 48*).

May Allah (SWT) grant us peace and tranquility of heart and spiritual elevation, and may He foster intense love in our hearts for Him and keep us steadfast on the truthful path that is pleasing to Him so that He loves us and never replaces us; and may He induce love in our hearts for our beloved Prophet (SAW) as well as for all believers and, indeed, for all of mankind with whom He is well-pleased; and may He grant us abundant sustenance from Himself that is a source of ever-recurring and rejuvenating happiness and contentment to us all as well as to our offspring, and may He make this a sign for us to remember Him and recognize His Majesty and to thank Him profusely, while never incurring His wrath through any form of ingratitude; and may He guide us to worship Him and perform acts of goodness toward humanity so that He then extends this sustenance multiplied several-fold for us in the Hereafter by His Grace and Mercy; and may He drive us to be humble and gentle toward believers and to strive against all forms of tyranny, oppression, discrimination, and censure; and may He unite us under the banner of His Own Party comprised of those who take as their solicitous friends Himself, His Messenger, as well as all believers who bow down to Him in submission and who keep up prayer along with acts of charity, for such are the ones who will triumph and succeed by His Grace and Mercy, which He gifts whomsoever He pleases, and He is Ample-giving, All-knowing, and the Best of Sustainers Ameen (*as inspired by the Qur'an, 5:54-56, 114-115*).

16

May Allah (SWT), to Whom belongs whatsoever is in the heavens and the earth, and whatever dwells in the night and the day, and Who feeds and is not fed, gift us graciously of His worldly as well as spiritual sustenance; and we ask Him Who has ordained mercy on Himself for mercy in the form that no one can grant but Him; and we reach out to Him longingly to be our Protecting Friend, Guide and Solicitor; and we implore Him to remove and avert any affliction from us for no one can do so but Him; and we beg Him to separate us from the disobedient ones who will incur His wrath on the Grievous Day, for indeed, anyone sheltered from grief on that day will be blessed by the mercy of the Almighty Lord; and we seek goodness from Him in this life and a manifest grand achievement in the Hereafter, for He is the Supreme, above His servants, and He is the Wise, the Aware, and the Possessor of Power over all things, Ameen (*as inspired by the Qur'an, 6:12-18*).

17

May Allah (SWT), the Originator of the heavens and the earth, the Self-subsisting One to Whom belongs all that is in the universe and Who feeds and sustains everyone and everything by day and by night, the sole-Knower of the unseen and the best-Knower of the seen that exists in the land and the sea, Who knows even the falling of a single leaf from a tree and a single grain in the darkness of the earth: guide us so that we serve no one besides Him, least of all our own low desires; and may He flourish our spirituality with beautified greenery and prevent it from drying up and withering; and may He grant us an honest and honorable sustenance during the day and direct our decisions moment to moment for He is the Best of Deciders; and may He grant our bodies and souls nourishment and success in this life and in the Hereafter and shower us with goodness from Himself and protect us and remove from us any affliction; and may He grant us peace in His companionship when He takes our souls at night while we sleep until He awakens us by His Will; and may He gift us with a state of intense peace when our term is fulfilled and He retains our souls; and may He honor us when He informs us of what we did and may He then join us with His beloved ones: the prophets, the truthful, the bearers of witness to the Truth, and the righteous, by His Grace and Mercy, for He has ordained mercy on Himself, and He is the Possessor of Power over all things, and He is indeed the Supreme, Wise, and Aware One Who looks benevolently well after His servants, Ameen (*as inspired by the Qur'an, 6:12-18, 56-60*).

18

May Allah (SWT), the Creator of the heavens and the earth, the Knower of the unseen and the seen, the Wise, the Aware the Supreme One Who is dominant above His servants, be a Compassionate and Merciful Keeper over us; and may He guide us, protect us, establish us, and shape our lives and our environment to be pleasing to Him; and may He assign His angels and righteous slaves to be our companions and support in all walks of life; and may He shelter us from His calamities and His wrath and chastisement that strike from the skies above us, or from the land beneath our feet; and may He prevent us from collapsing into confusion, or splitting into disunited parties, or tasting in the least bit the violence of others; and may He withdraw us from those who defile our religion; and may He partition us from those who have been deceived by the life of this world and who take the Word of Allah (SWT) as a play and an idle sport, for indeed, besides Him we have no protecting friend, solicitor, or intercessor; and may He make us upright and enable us to turn ourselves wholly to Him alone in devoted submission, ascribing no partners to Him in any form or manner, for when He so intends and declares in response to our plea, "Be", then, and only then, will it come to pass, by His Grace and Mercy, Ameen (*as inspired by the Qur'an, 6:61-70, 73-74, 80*).

May Allah (SWT) bring to fruition and successful completion all our endeavors in a manner that is pleasing to Him, much like He sends down water from the clouds and causes the grain and seed to germinate and flourish; and may He guide us steadfastly along the path of Truth through the Glorious Qur'an and the enlightened teachings of the Prophet (SAW), as well as through His angels and His righteous learned slaves, much like He has made the sun and the moon for reckoning and He has made the stars so that we might follow the right way thereby in the darkness of the land and the sea; and may He purify our faith and beautify and enlighten our worship of Him, ascribing no partners to Him; and may He induce our efforts and sacrifices to be done for no one or no motive except for Him alone; and may He shape every aspect and moment of our life until the time that we return to Him in a fashion that pleases and honors Him to the highest degree, so that our prayers and our sacrifice and our life and our death are all most sincerely and surely for our Creator, Allah (SWT), for nothing less befits the Supreme Lord of all the Worlds, and He is truly the Exalted, Magnified One, solely worthy of glorification, Ameen (*as inspired by the Qur'an, 6:96-101, 163*).

20

May Allah (SWT) enable us to take a firm hold of the lifeline of support He has gifted us with, the Qur'an, and be abundantly grateful to Him for this precious Message He has bountifully graced us with by His Benevolent Mercy; and may He make us of the *Muttakeen* (the God conscious ones) and the *Muhsineeen* (the doers of good to others); and may He prohibit even an iota of pride in our hearts so that we are ever in His remembrance and submissive to Him in humility; and may He sharpen our spiritual sight so that we clearly recognize even the mildest of signs from Him and see with clarity the right path of rectitude; and may He steer us away from the many deceitful paths of error that lead to damnation; and may He establish an impenetrable barrier between us and the ones who reject His messages and are heedless of them and who, if they see the way of rectitude, they take it not for a way, and if they see the way of error, they take it for a way, for indeed, we would be lost if the Almighty Lord leaves our hand even for the twinkling of an eye, Ameen (*as inspired by the Qur'an, 7:144-146*).

21

We ask Allah (SWT) to forgive us and to admit us unto His Mercy by His Grace, for He is the Best of those who forgive and the Most Merciful of those who show mercy; and we ask Him to guide and protect us and to shield us from the evil ways of those who have gone astray, for surely we would perish without the constant guidance and company of the Almighty Lord of the heavens and the earth; and we plead with Him to ordain for us goodness in this life and in the Hereafter by virtue of turning us toward those who truly believe in His message and who honor and follow and help in propagating the illuminating light sent through His beloved Prophet (SAW); and who keep their duty and retain consciousness of His Presence moment-to-moment; and who perform acts of charity in all its forms, including enjoining what is right and forbidding what is wrong; and who enjoy the good and lawful things that they have been provided with by their Lord and shun the harmful and impure things, for indeed such are the ones from whom the burdening shackles of fear and grief are lifted, and who are among the successful ones who earn the pleasure of their Creator, the Most High, Ameen (*as inspired by the Qur'an, 7:151-157*).

In the Name of Allah, the Beneficent, the Merciful

22

May Allah (SWT) guide us and foster piety in us and enhance our *Taqwa*, God consciousness, by bringing us closer to Him; and may He enable us to uphold our duty to Him in due reverence and perfection with obedience, responsibility, and gratitude, so that He may thereby confer upon us the true distinction of being a *Muhmin* (deeply genuine believer) among Muslims; and may He purify us by blotting out our misguided evil inclinations, and protect us from wrongdoings, and forgive us for our shortcomings, and assist us in all walks of life, and guide our decisions and formulate our plans in the best of manner such that it benefits us abundantly, both in the life of this world and in the Hereafter, for surely He is the best of Planners; and above all, may He be our Eternal Patron, for indeed, He is the most excellent Patron and the most excellent Helper, and He is truly the Lord of Mighty Grace, Most Merciful to His servants, Ameen (*as inspired by the Qur'an, 8:29-30, 40*).

23

May Allah (SWT) relieve and bring solace to our hearts and gift us with the most intimate friendship, that of Himself and His beloved Messenger, and make our hearts hold nothing dearer than this; and may He keep us always in the company of true believers, and remove the rage in the hearts of those who unwittingly and unfairly oppose us and, instead, replace it with benevolence towards us; and may He enable us to strive hard and struggle in His path with our wealth and our lives, keep up acts of beautified worship and charity, and fear none but Him, so that we rise in rank in His Eyes and earn the good news of Mercy and Pleasure from Himself, along with abundant blessings and eternal bliss in Gardens that He has promised by His Grace and Mercy, for He is indeed the Wise, All-Knowing, and Aware One Who has ordained Mercy on Himself, Ameen (*as inspired by the Qur'an, 9:14-16, 18, 20-24*).

24

May Allah (SWT) grant us peace and the invaluable gift of guidance along the *Siraat-ul-Mustakeem* (the right path of Truth), and may He purify our thoughts, words, and actions so that we worship Him, and Him alone, with devotion and reverence in a manner that befits His Majesty and Glory; and that we carry the torch of Islam to enlighten the world through our deeds and efforts so that we neutralize those who desire to put out the light of Allah (SWT), although they can never do so for He will allow nothing except the perfection of His light and for the Religion of Truth to prevail over all other forms of beliefs and religions, regardless of the struggle to the contrary by those who are averse; and may He protect us from falsely devouring the property of others and from hoarding wealth without sharing it generously with those in need, for indeed on the awesome Day of Reckoning, such hoarded wealth will be heated in the fire of Hell, and the foreheads and sides of the hoarders will be branded with it, may the Almighty Lord forbid this of us; and may He make us content with what He has given us, and may He clarify our sight to recognize Him as being sufficient for us, so that then, as promised, He will grant us more out of His Grace, for He is the Most Generous, Most Gracious, Most Merciful One, Ameen (*as inspired by the Qur'an, 9:31-35,59*).

25

May Allah (SWT) grant us the friendship of true, righteous believers and foster unity among us with love and compassion for each other; and may He guide us so that we unwaveringly obey Him and His Messenger, and we enjoin and encourage what is right and forbid and repel what is wrong, and we establish prayer with sincerity and devotion, and we perform acts of charity with love and tenderness in our hearts toward all of mankind; and may He shelter us from any form of wrongdoings and from those who enjoin evil and forbid good and withhold their hands from giving; and may He enable us to strive hard with our property and our persons, and not fear the going forth in His way through the heat of hardships, for indeed the Fire of Hell is fiercer in heat; and may He count us among such successful people who have earned His mercy and have attained the *great achievement* of inheriting blissful Gardens of perpetual abode wherein rivers flow, dwelling in magnificent mansions, and more so, who have attained the incomparably *grand achievement* of earning the unsurpassably precious gift of the Goodly Pleasure of the Almighty Lord, the Most Wise, by His coveted Grace and Mercy, Ameen (*as inspired by the Qur'an 9:67, 71-72, 81, 88-89*).

26

We turn in complete surrender and submission to our Creator, the Almighty Lord to Whom belongs the Kingdom of the heavens and the earth, and Who gives life and causes death, both physically and spiritually, and besides Whom we have no friend nor helper, and we ask Him to turn to us in mercy and to guide and cultivate us so that we are among those true believers who serve Him and praise Him and worship Him; and who fast with their entire being and with all their senses; and who bow down and prostrate themselves fervently and abundantly while knowing that it is yet insufficient from what He truly deserves; and who enjoin what is good and forbid what is evil in order to encourage others as well along this righteous path, for it is no doubt their duty to do so; and who keep within the limits and boundaries set by their Creator and Master; and we surrender to Him our persons and our property in return for the mighty achievement of the Eternal Garden in His Overwhelming Presence in the bliss of Jannah, which He has promised in the Torah and the Gospel and the Qur'an, and we rejoice in this bargain that He has made binding on Himself, for who else is more faithful to his promise than Allah (SWT), the Most Compassionate, Most Merciful One, Ameen (*as inspired by the Qur'an, 9:111-112, 116-117*).

27

We extend our deepest love and most sincere salutations of peace and blessings to our beloved Prophet Muhammad (SAW), who grieves for us when we fall into distress or indulge in wrongdoings, and who is solicitous for us in front of our Almighty Lord, and who, we hope, will Insha'Allah intercede favorably on our behalf on the Day of Judgment, and with whom Allah (SWT) has shared His very Own titles of being compassionate and merciful; and we likewise send peace and blessings on his household and his family and his entire *Ummah*; and we turn to Allah (SWT), the Creator of the heavens and the earth Who is established on the Throne of Power regulating all affairs, and we ask Him to strengthen our belief and enhance our *Taqwa* and enable us to serve Him by performing beautiful acts of goodness so that we advance in excellence in His estimation; and we plead with Him to guide us by our induced faith so that our light runs before us as we progress to our meeting with Him; and we fervently hope that He will be well-pleased with us when we stand before Him, and will grant us Gardens of bliss under which rivers flow, where our cry is, "Glory be to Thee, O Allah!", and our greeting is simply, "Peace!", and our ultimate declaration is, "Praise and thanks be to Allah, the Lord of all the worlds!", by His Grace and Mercy, for He is the One and Only Supreme Creator, Nourisher, Sustainer, Enactor, and the Lord of the Mighty Throne on Whom alone we rely, and He is indeed sufficient for us, Ameen (*as inspired by the Qur'an, 9:128-129; 10:2-3, 9-10*).

28

We ask Allah (SWT), the True Lord Who guides to the Truth, and Who controls the hearing and the sight, and Who brings forth the living from the dead and the dead from the living, and Who gives sustenance from the heavens and the earth, and Who creates the first creation and then reproduces it, and Who regulates the affair: to guide us and shelter us from the spiritually deaf and the blind who are lost and cannot find a way without being themselves guided; and to grant us peace and protection and solace and bliss under His Loving Care; and to give us wisdom and light and to bring the spiritually dead to life and to prevent us from spiritual death after He has given us life; and to provide us sustenance from Himself along with contentment with what He has apportioned for us; and to manage and regulate all our affairs and set a straight course in them, for there is no one but Him, the Supreme One, Who can do this, by His Grace and Mercy, Ameen (*as inspired by the Qur'an, 10:31-35*).

29

We ask Allah (SWT) for spiritual life and sustenance and an uplifted heart that finds solace in having earned His Pleasure; and we entreat Him for protection from the day when every soul that has done injustice will express intense regret and will offer in ransom all that is in the earth were it in his possession; and we beseech our Creator and Rabb to grant us an enriched spiritual life and sustenance, for surely whatever is in the heavens and the earth is His; and we fervently seek guidance from Him through what He has revealed in the Glorious Qur'an so that we heed its admonition and fully embrace its laws and injunctions such that it heals any defect in our hearts; and we deeply thank Him for this bountiful gift and we rejoice in His Grace and Mercy, which He has promised us thereby and which is far better than the material wealth that the lost ones hoard, for surely His promise is indeed true, Ameen (*as inspired by the Qur'an, 10:54-60*).

30

May Allah (SWT) erase and prevent any doubt in our hearts pertaining to the True Religion that He has gifted us by His Grace and Mercy, and may He enable us to set our purpose towards it uprightly and to serve Him along this path wholeheartedly and exclusively with patience and piety and spiritual bliss, calling on Him alone, for there is nothing or no one else that can either benefit or harm us; and we plead with Him to remove and shelter us from any harmful affliction, for there is no one that can do so but He; and we ask Him to guide us to the pure Truth and to let us see with clarity of all senses that whoever goes aright does so for the good of his own soul, and whoever errs does so only against his own soul; and we beg Him for this and all forms of goodness, for there is none to repel the Grace that He intends to bestow upon whomsoever He pleases, and indeed, He is the Best of judges and He is the Most Forgiving, Merciful, Ameen (*as inspired by the Qur'an, 10:104-109*).

In the Name of Allah, the Beneficent, the Merciful

31

May Allah (SWT) always keep us in a state of total awareness, through all our senses, of His immense mercy and favors upon us; and may He make us patient in distress and thankful when He alleviates us of such trials by His Grace and Mercy, unlike those who are blind and deaf and unaware of His mercy except when it is withdrawn from them, whence they are despairing, ungrateful, and who, when their Lord gives them a taste of favor after distress has afflicted them, are boastful and exultant; and may He grant us humility and make us of the doers of good to humanity who constantly seek His forgiveness and turn to Him, for such are the ones on whom He will bestow a goodly provision and grace in the life of this world, and whom He will endow with incomparable grace and mercy in the Hereafter, making them owners of the sublime Gardens wherein they will abide; indeed, to Him is our return and He is the Wise, the Aware, and the Possessor of Power over all things, Ameen (*as inspired by the Qur'an, 11:1,3-4, 9-11, 23-24*).

32

May Allah (SWT) be ever watchful over us and may He guide us in every step we take and in every journey we embark on and every task we undertake, so that in His Glorified Name be its sailing and its anchoring, its beginning and its end; and may we transition through life under His Mindful Eyes, and may He cultivate desires in our hearts and plant supplications on our tongues of only that which He wills and which is pleasing to Him and is cherished by us; and may He grant us refuge in Himself from asking of Him that of which we have no knowledge, or lack the wisdom to recognize its detrimental effects; for unless He forgives our shortcomings and has mercy on us, we shall surely be among the losers; yet, notwithstanding this fear, may our hearts find hope and solace in knowing that, surely, our Lord is Most Forgiving, Most Merciful, Ameen (*as inspired by the Qur'an, 11:41, 47*).

33

May Allah (SWT) strengthen our hearts with His Divine Message, and enlighten us with the Truth that He has revealed, and make us take heed of His admonitions and warnings; and may He enable us to turn to Him and to keep steadfastly on the right path as we are commanded; and may He protect us from being inordinate and from inclining in the slightest to the unjust ones who do wrong and who mindlessly pursue the enjoyment of plenty, lest the fire touches us, even barely, with proximity to them, for then we shall have no protectors besides Allah (SWT) and no one to assist us; and may He guide us to keep up prayer along with the performance of good deeds that more than erase any wrongdoing and, beyond this, to purify ourselves further, and to act well, to enjoin what is right and forbid what is wrong, to put our complete trust in Him and to serve Him – all this so as to earn His Protection and His Grace and Mercy, for indeed, He is heedful of what we do, and to Him belongs the seen and the unseen of the heavens and the earth, and to Him will everyone, everything, and every affair return, and surely, He will aptly reward the doers of good, Ameen (*as inspired by the Qur'an, 11:112-123*).

34

May Allah (SWT) grant us forgiveness and protect us from our human propensity to commit sins; and may He sharpen our conscience to feel the pangs of even the slightest departure from the path of rectitude that He has so graciously revealed to us; and may He raise our souls and spirits to be at peace and rest in His remembrance and obedience; and may He guide us to the right religion and shape our intentions and actions to serve Him alone, ascribing no partners to Him; and may He enlighten us to be thankful to Him for His Grace upon us and upon all of mankind for showing us the path of proper worship, and for His immense Mercy by which He judges us thereby, Ameen (*as inspired by the Qur'an, 12:38-40, 52-53*).

35

We acknowledge and thank the Almighty Lord, Allah (SWT), the Grand Originator of the heavens and the earth and all that is in-between, and the Supreme Disposer of all Affairs, for His innumerable gifts that permeate our entire being and exist all around us, including a multitude of such gifts that we are even unaware of and oblivious to, and for His kindness and the physical and spiritual sustenance that He has so graciously bestowed upon us from His vast kingdom; and we express our grief and sorrow only to Him, the Most High, and entreat Him to grant us contentment with what He has willed for us, and to gift us with *Sabr Jameel* – goodly patience, for indeed He is the ultimate *Al-Sabur* – the All Patient One; and we ask for blessings for our loved ones whom we recognize just by their touch, as well as for our dear departed ones whom we remember even by their scent; and we beseech Him to never let us despair of His mercy, for surely, none despairs of His mercy except the disbelieving people; and we plead with Him to plan favorably for us with loving, meticulous care that only He can provide; and we call on Him and yearn for Him to be our Benignant Protecting Friend, Guide, Solicitor, and Enactor in this world and in the Hereafter, and we beg Him to hold our hands and to not let go, and to make us die in complete submission to Him alone, and to join us with His most beloved righteous ones with whom He is well-pleased, by His Grace and Mercy, for truly, He is All Knowing and Wise, and the Most Forgiving and Merciful One Who loves to forgive, Ameen (*as inspired by the Qur'an, 12:76, 83, 86-87, 93, 98, 100-101*).

36

May Allah (SWT), the Knower of the seen and the unseen, the Great, the Most High, to Whom make obeisance whoever is in the heavens and the earth, willingly or unwillingly, and their shadows too, morning and evening, and to Whom true prayer is due, and Whose praises are celebrated by thunder and lightning and all elements and phenomena of the universe and by the angels too in utter awe of Him: guide us to purify our worship of Him, and Him alone, and not be like the disbeliever who stretches forth his hands towards water so that perchance it might reach his mouth, although it never will since his prayer is only wasted; and may He enlighten us and enable us to see the truth clearly and to perform magnificent acts of goodness that are everlasting and that benefit the lives of all people, unlike the acts of the spiritually blind ones who grope in darkness and whose acts are like the scum of melted ornaments that passes away as worthless waste; and may He protect us from those who mean us harm, either openly by their words and actions or in a concealed manner behind our backs; and may He assign His angels by His Command to guard us, before us and behind us; and may He rectify our ways to be ever turning to Him devotedly, so that He modifies our condition constantly for the better; and may He make us hear and respond to His call and not be like the deaf ones who are heedless of Him until they face Him on the Day of Judgement, whence they will be willing to offer as ransom all that is in the earth and the like thereof along with it if they so possessed it; and may He bestow on us the spiritual blessing of abundantly flowing water, all by His Benevolent Grace and Mercy, Ameen (*as inspired by the Qur'an, 13:9-18*).

37

May Allah (SWT) enhance our understanding of His revelations and help us uphold them with awe of Him as He truly deserves; and may He prevent us from being distracted and misled by the transitory life of this world, which is only a temporary enjoyment as compared with the Hereafter; and may He enable us to fulfil our pacts and covenants that we have made with Him and with His creatures, and may He direct us to not cut asunder the ties of love and relationships that He has commanded to be joined; and may He amplify our physical and spiritual sustenance by His Pleasure; and may He induce us to be steadfast and constant in seeking His pleasure while keeping up with prayer and performing all kinds of acts of charity, and repelling and amending evil with goodness; and may He, by His benevolent Grace and Mercy, admit us to the highest level of Gardens of Perpetuity along with our loved ones, where angels enter upon us from every gate and greet us with the blessings of peace on account of our constancy and perseverance in loving and seeking the pleasure of our Lord and Creator; indeed, how excellent is such a final abode! Ameen (*as inspired by the Qur'an, 13:19-26*).

38

May Allah (SWT) always turn us toward Himself and bestow on us His most gracious gift of guidance; and may He make His message of the Glorious Qur'an cleave our hearts and enter deep within it, much as the earth is cloven asunder by deep roots; and may He enrich our hearts with tranquility in His remembrance, for indeed, in the remembrance of Allah (SWT) do hearts find rest; and may He remove, and grant us ease from, the formidable mountain-like obstacles we face that only He can make to pass away; and may He clean our hearts of even a modicum of doubt in His revelations and promise, and instead fill it with total and complete belief and trust in Him; and may He enable us to accompany this unwavering belief with beautiful acts of goodness toward all of mankind; and may He facilitate for us a goodly return to Him and a magnificent final state by His Grace and Mercy, for surely the commandment is wholly Allah's and His Promise is true, Ameen (*as inspired by the Qur'an, 13:27-31*).

39

May Allah (SWT), the Mighty One deserving the Highest Praises, keep us in the Light of Islam to which He has most graciously guided us, and may He shun darkness and ignorance from our hearts and our lives; and may He always steer us toward the straight path and keep us steadfast therein and never leave us in a state of misguided error; and may He imbibe in us a far greater love for the Hereafter than for the life of this world; and may He grant us the sustenance He has destined for us with ease and make us ever grateful to Him for the favors He has conferred upon us and make us content thereby, for to Him belongs whatsoever is in the heavens and the earth, and He is the Mighty, the Wise, Ameen (*as inspired by the Qur'an, 14:1-5*).

40

May Allah (SWT) sow the seeds of His Good Word through us so that our deeds blossom like a tree that is watered by the gift of true faith, and whose roots are firm and whose branches are high, yielding fruits in every season and thereby bringing joy and pleasure to our Lord and to all of humankind; and we ask Him to steer us clear from the evil word that is like a shriveled, uprooted tree that bears no fruit and has no stability; and we ask Him to protect us from the accursed, slinking *Shaitaan* who has no authority over man except that he calls him to evil and the blameworthy person obeys him, for surely, the promise of the devil is false whereas the promise of Allah (SWT) is true; and may He fulfill His promised Word of assurance for us in the life of this world and in the Hereafter, and by His permission, and His Grace and Mercy, admit us to Gardens wherein rivers flow and fruit-bearing trees thrive, fittingly reflecting the good acts of its inhabitants, and may our greeting therein, in a state of sublime peace, be simply, "Peace!", Ameen (*as inspired by the Qur'an, 14:22-27*).

41

We gratefully bow our heads in thanks to the Lord of the Mighty Throne, Who has created the heavens and the earth in varied hues by His Power and Magnificence and has made it subservient to us, and Who sends down water from the clouds for us to drink and to nourish the plants and trees that produce sumptuous sustenance that we delight in eating, and Who has created the sun and the moon and the stars, each pursuing its course, by which we work and rest and measure time and find our way, and the vast seas that provide fresh nourishment for us as well as a means of travel to seek His bounties, and the mountains that balance the smooth rotation of the earth, and the rivers and roads and landmarks by which we find our way to traverse this beautiful world, for indeed, if we were to even dare to count and enumerate the multitude of favors of our Creator we would fail ever so miserably; and we ask Allah (SWT) for His invaluable guidance so that we might be His righteous servants who reflect, and understand, and remain mindful, and give profuse thanks, and keep up devotional prayers, and spend generously out of that which He has gifted us, and perform acts of overarching goodness toward all, before there comes the day when there will be no bartering or befriending, whence we hope and pray for His forgiveness and mercy, for He is assuredly the Most Forgiving, Most Gracious, Most Merciful, Ameen (*as inspired by the Qur'an, 14:31-34, 16:10-20*).

May Allah (SWT) enable us to establish prayer in a state of spiritual bliss and in the delightful company of His angels and righteous slaves, worshipping Him alone with due devotion and mindful concentration, and may He accept it from us; and may He grant us and our families and the righteous believers protection and security in the life of this world and on the day when the reckoning comes to pass; and may He turn the hearts of all to yearn with love towards us; and may He bestow on us productivity in our actions and gift us from Himself nourishment for our bodies and for our souls; and may He purify our hearts, enlighten our minds, and cleanse our souls, for surely He knows what we hide and what we proclaim and nothing is hidden from Him in the earth or in the heaven; indeed, He is the Most Forgiving, Merciful One, and the Hearer of prayer, Ameen (*as inspired by the Qur'an, 14:35-41*).

We ask Allah (SWT), Who created us of sounding clay, of black mud fashioned into shape, to grant us humility as per our origin and our final state of life back to dust, and to make our gift of speech pure and truthful so that we are deserving of the Holy Spirit that He breathed into us from Himself upon our creation; and we beseech Him to protect us from the evil inclinations of the *Shaitaan* who refused to bow to us; and we implore Him to let us be among His purified, righteous servants who follow the right way and over whom the accursed devil has no authority whatsoever to deviate an digress from the Truth or to make evil fair-seeming; and we entreat Him to keep us united and remove any rancor in our hearts toward our fellow Muslims, and to grant us forgiveness when we slip and stray from His directed path and to never let us despair of His Benevolent Mercy, for who despairs of the mercy of his Lord except the erring ones; and we beg Him to let us be among the dutiful ones whom He admits by His Grace and Mercy into Gardens with rivers and fountains, in absolute peace and security and restful joy, for indeed He is the Most Loving, Forgiving, Merciful; Ameen (*as inspired by the Qur'an, 15: 26-29, 39-42, 45-49, 55-56*).

44

We ask Allah (SWT), Who created the heavens and the earth in Truth and Who knows, controls, and sustains it all, to guide us unwaveringly with the Glorious Qur'an and its magnificent opening seven oft-repeated verses; and we ask Him to elevate our souls so that we are gentle towards our fellow believers and that we turn away from the hurtful ones with kindly forgiveness, for the Hour is surely imminent, whence we ourselves will yearn for forgiveness from the Master of the Day of Judgement and will seek His Love and Mercy; and we ask Him to grant us understanding of His Will and Purpose, as also contentment with what He has apportioned for us, so that we do not strain our eyes at what He has given certain classes of people as a means of trial for them; and we ask Him to alleviate us of any form of fear or grief or straitness of the heart, and to instill in us the faith and trust that He is sufficient for us against any miscreants or scoffers; and we implore Him to immerse us in His remembrance so that we celebrate His praises and serve Him and make obeisance to Him moment to moment, until there comes to us that which is certain, and to beautify our souls when we eventually return to Him, Ameen (*as inspired by the Qur'an, 15:85-88, 95, 97-99*).

45

May Allah (SWT), Who is all Good, induce His Goodness in us so that we worship Him as He deserves to be worshipped, and we keep our duty to Him and serve Him with a joyous heart by performing good deeds towards all, so that when we leave this world, the angels cause us to die in purity with a greeting of peace upon us; and may He then admit us into exquisite Gardens of perpetuity, wherein flow rivers and we have therein what we please, for certainly the abode of the Hereafter is better, an apt reward indeed for those who keep their duty to their Creator and who do good in this world, all by His Grace and Mercy, Ameen (*as inspired by the Qur'an, 16:30-32*).

46

May Allah (SWT) grant us guidance and spiritual and moral elevation and goodness, despite the decadence and immorality that surrounds us, just as He produces the pure and nourishing drink of milk in cattle, separating the nutrients within the putrid feces in the intestines through the flow of blood; and may He enable us to adopt His Word of the Glorious Qur'an and the teachings of His most illustrious Prophet (SAW) in its pure and absolutely beautiful original form without any adulterations, just as in the physical world, He has produced the delicious fruits of the palms and the grapes to nourish us, and He has thankfully sheltered us from the foolish ones who ferment these into despicable intoxicants; and may He instill in us love and appreciation for our beloved Prophet Muhammad (SAW), who collected the Divine Word of his Creator and delivered it to us, both through the Glorious Qur'an and by virtue of his spiritually inspired teachings and practices comprising his *Sunnah*, in order to cure us of our spiritual diseases, just as Allah (SWT) inspired the bees to build hives and eat the fruits and collect the nectar of flowers to produce thereby the various exquisite types of honey, all of which provide healing for our ailments in the physical world; and may He preserve us in our minds and bodies and souls so that we do not decay into worthlessness, knowing nothing after having the knowledge that He has gifted us with, by His Grace and Mercy, for surely He is the All Knowing, the Powerful, Ameen (*as inspired by the Qur'an, 16: 66-70*).

In the Name of Allah, the Beneficent, the Merciful

47

May Allah (SWT) envelope us with His Goodness and endow us with high moral and spiritual values that are pleasing to Him, so that we enjoin justice and the doing of good, perform acts of kindness towards our kindred as well as towards all His creations, and uphold our promises and covenants as inviolable sacred obligations; and may He unite all Muslims as a single nation with solidarity and make us a shining beacon of goodness for all of humankind; and may He grant us refuge from the accursed devil and never let him have even an inkling of authority over us; and may He protect us from any acts of indecency, evil, or rebellion, keeping us ever mindful of His Presence in our midst and in our very being; and may He preserve our acts of goodness so that we don't unravel them and let them slip away, like one who has spun a yarn strongly and then disintegrates it senselessly; and may He grant us a good life in this world with patience in all our dealings, realizing that the transitory things of life will pass away, but that which we send forward to our Lord with goodness will endure; and on the day when He raises us to stand before Him and He brings our beloved Prophet (SAW) as a witness before us, may He render us worthy of that meeting and forgive and hide our shortcomings and mistakes, and may He reward us abundantly for the best of what we did, all by His immense Grace and Mercy, Ameen (*as inspired by the Qur'an, 16:89-100*).

48

May Allah (SWT) grant us the nobility of character and virtues that he gifted His beloved Prophet Muhammad (SAW) and His beloved *Khaleel* Ibraheem (AS), and may He guide us towards righteousness and enable us to adopt their model of virtue, being obedient to Him, grateful for His innumerable favors, and ascribing no partners to Him in any form or manner, so that He gives us thereby an abundance of good in this world as well as in the Hereafter; and may He shine His light through us so that we induce this nobility of character in others, inviting and calling mankind to the way of our Lord with wisdom and goodly exhortation in the best possible fashion; and may He grant us patience in all our endeavors and not let us fall into despair or distress, for surely, He is with those who are pious and who keep their duty and do good to others, and He is the Most Gracious, Most Merciful, Ameen (*as inspired by the Qur'an, 16:120-122, 125, 127-128*).

In the Name of Allah, the Beneficent, the Merciful

49

May Allah (SWT) Inspire in us supplications that are beneficial to us, and may He prevent us from hastily asking of that which is harmful to us or of which we have no knowledge; and may He remove the ignorance of darkness from us and enlighten us, just as He makes the night to pass away and reveals the glorious brightness of day for us to seek of His bountiful Grace; and may He guide us and purify our faith to worship Him alone and thereby prevent us from ever being despised or forsaken; and may He make our actions noble so that we receive our book of deeds on the day we meet Him in our right hand and with joy, for indeed, whoever goes aright does so for his own soul, and whoever goes astray does so for his own detriment, and no one will bear the burden of another in this regard; and may He instill in our souls true belief and *Imaan*, and infuse in our hearts the desire for the Hereafter and enable us to strive for it as we ought to strive, and may He remove from our hearts any worthless desires pertaining only to the transitory life of our existence in this world, for surely the Hereafter is greater in degrees and greater in excellence, and the bounty of our Lord is not limited and He gives it to whomsoever He wills as He pleases, and He is the Most Bountiful and Gracious, Most Forgiving and Merciful, Ameen (*as inspired by the Qur'an, 17:11-22*).

50

We ask Allah (SWT) to bless our parents and to have mercy on them, and to enable us to serve them well and to be good and kind and gentle towards them, and to lower to them the wing of humility as they did for us, bringing us up when we were little; and we ask Him to purify and sanctify our souls and hearts with righteousness and morality, so that we give to the near of kin and the needy with humility, gentleness and a kind word, and we waste not or squander the resources He has gifted us, nor do we hoard it with our hands shackled to our necks; and we deprive not our families and our offspring of the sustenance we have been blessed with, and we provide both worldly and spiritual education to them; and we guard against evil and indecent acts, and treat the gift of life granted to people by our Creator as sacred and inviolable within the scope of justice; and we respect the property of people and tend toward the needs of orphans and the helpless ones; and we earn an honest livelihood and give due measure and weight and service in all our dealings; and we follow not falsely that of which we have no knowledge, conjecturing and speculating and gossiping and hurting the hearts of innocent ones, for surely the hearing and the sight and the hearts will all be asked to account for their actions; and we go not about the land exulting with pride, for indeed we cannot rend asunder the earth nor can we reach the stature of mountains; and we ask Allah (SWT) for wisdom from Himself and, most of all, we ask Him to purify our *Imaan* so that we worship Him alone and put our complete trust in Him wholeheartedly, all by His Grace and Mercy, Ameen (*as inspired by the Qur'an, 17:23-39*).

51

May Allah (SWT) always envelope us with His Loving Care and keep us under the shade of His Mighty Throne and be ever close to us; and may He grant us honor and make us excel all His creations and provide us with goodness that is beneficial to us in the life of this world and that reaps magnificent rewards in the Hereafter; and may He grant us protection and security, and keep our hearts in constant remembrance of Him, both in times of hardship and ease, with immense gratitude for all His innumerable favors, for He is the Most Gracious Sustainer and there is none but Him who can remove distress when it afflicts us and who can keep us secure from disasters; and may the Almighty Creator grant us protection and security against the machinations of the *Shaitaan* who incites man with his whisperings and suggestions, and tempts with illegitimate desires and promises of pleasure and the glitter of illegally acquired wealth; and may Allah (SWT) gift us with the clarity of sight and mind to realize that the promises of the devil are only meant to deceive, whereas the true promise of success lies in attaining the pleasure of our Lord, the Most High, and may we excel in this, by His Grace and Mercy, Ameen (*as inspired by the Qur'an, 17:64-70*).

52

We glorify, and magnify, and proclaim the Incomparable Greatness of Allah (SWT), the Most Beneficent and Merciful One to Whom all Praise is due, and Who has no partners whatsoever in His Kingdom and Who needs no help, and Who is the Great Knower of the seen and the unseen, and Who is the *Al-Haqq*, The Absolute Truth, Who sent His beloved Prophet (SAW) to establish Truth on earth, for indeed the Truth has come and has vanquished falsehood and has enslaved it so that it shall never prevail or reproduce, but is ever bound to vanish, and Who has revealed His Word, The Magnificent Qur'an, in purified pages of Truth, and we plead with Him to assist and support and guide us, and to let the Qur'an be a source of healing for the ailments of our souls, our bodies, our hearts and our spirit, and to let it enter and occupy and fill our hearts and be an ever flowing stream of His Benevolence upon us; and we implore Him to enable us to appreciate, understand, and follow its enlightened guidance in every walk of our lives in due reverence; and we beseech Him to make its messages inspire us and stir our emotions so that we fall prostrate in humility, weeping, begging for HIs Love, Forgiveness, Grace and Mercy; and we entreat Him to direct our pathways so that our entry into every place or affair is a blessed and truthful one, and our exit from the place or affair is a blessed and truthful one with an honorable mention, and we seek His invaluable guidance and support during our tenure in the place or involvement in the affair by virtue of His own ever-Caring Presence and Absolute Authority, whilst in the company of His angels and righteous servants; and we recognize that His promise for forgiveness and mercy in return for our sincere submission is true, and we yearn for the fulfillment of this promise in favor of us moment-to-moment until we stand in judgement before Him, and beyond, Ameen (*as inspired by the Qur'an, 17:80-82; 105-111; 34:48-49*).

53

We ask Allah (SWT), to Whom belongs the seen and the unseen of the heavens and the earth, and Who knows the minutest aspect of the entire universe - indeed, how clear is His sight and His hearing, and besides Whom there is no guardian or refuge, and there is none who can alter His words or associate with Him in His judgement: to grant us mercy from Himself and to direct a right and profitable course in all our affairs and plans, which facilitates a favorable and successful outcome that is pleasing to Him and with which we are well-pleased; and we entreat Him to grant us humility and enable us to recognize that the Truth and Will of Purpose are from Him alone and that there is no power except in Him, and we seek His forgiveness and His assistance in rectifying our course of action to a more righteous one if we forget or make a mistake; and we beseech Him to keep us in the company of those who call on their Lord morning and evening, desiring His goodwill, and to not even let our eyes pass from them, desiring the beauty of this world's life, and we plead with Him to shelter and separate us from the one who follows his own low desires and whose heart has been rendered devoid and unmindful of the remembrance of his Lord because he has exceeded due bounds; and we implore Him to guide us and make us of those who believe and do good works and whose reward is not wasted but is preserved and that blossoms into Gardens of perpetuity wherein flow rivers, and who are adorned therein reflectively with bracelets of gold and given to wear green robes of fine silk and thick brocade, reclining on raised couches - indeed, how excellent the recompense and goodly the resting place, all by the Grace and Mercy of the Almighty Lord, the Most High, Ameen (*as inspired by the Qur'an, 18: 10, 16, 23-24, 26-31, 34, 39*).

54

May Allah (SWT) guide us and imbibe in us the proper understanding and perspective of the life of this world and its adornments of wealth and possessions, which flourish as per the will and control of the Almighty Lord, Who has power over all things, but become dry and break into pieces that the winds scatter by His Will and Purpose, and that it is the good works that are better and ever-abiding, and it is the Hereafter of which the outcomes are more definitive and much better to hope for; and may He keep us always mindful of the day when the obstacles to the Truth and the magnificence of the mountains will pass away and the earth will become a levelled plain, and men will be brought before their Creator, some even bewildered that there was an appointment made for them with their Lord, and their book of deeds will be placed before them, confronting them, some fearing its contents and others rejoicing thereat, for it will leave out neither a small thing nor a great one, but will enumerate them all; and may He grant us patience and perseverance as we progress toward that Day, for indeed, we find it formidable to have patience in that whereof we lack a comprehensive knowledge, so we implore this of Him, by His immense Grace and Mercy, Ameen (*as inspired by the Qur'an, 18:45-49, 68*).

55

We express our sincere desire to Allah (SWT) for His endearing love and constant support, crying to Him in secret, and may He never leave us unblessed or unsuccessful in our prayers; and may He guide us to take hold of His Glorious revelations with strength and constancy and wisdom; and may He make us kind-hearted and dutiful towards all and purify us and shelter us from any form of insolence or disobedience; and may He grant us benevolence towards our parents and forgive them and have mercy on them and gift them abundantly for their love and mercy towards us; and may He grant us peace on the day that we were born, and peace and joy on the day that we return to Him, and peace and bliss on the day we are raised again to face Him, standing before Him all alone by ourselves; and may He enable us to prepare well for that day so that it is not a Day of Regret for us as it will be for the disbelievers and evil-doers who are driven to His fearful chastisement like thirsty beasts, but instead, we implore Him to make us of those who believe and do good deeds so that the Day of Reckoning becomes one of receiving honors from Him and a day on which the Almighty Lord brings about love for us, by His incomparable Beneficence, Grace, and Mercy, Ameen (*as inspired by the Qur'an, 19:3-4, 12-15, 32-33, 39-40, 43-50, 85-86, 95-96*).

56

May Allah (SWT), the One Who creates and then guides, gift us with guidance from Himself in all walks of life and may He blanket us with peace thereby; and may He choose us for Himself and shower His love on us and direct our lives before His Eyes so that our own eyes might be cooled thereby; and may He enable us to remember and glorify Him moment-to-moment as He deserves, and never make us remiss thereby; and may He expand our breast with His guidance and loosen the knot in our tongues and purify our actions so that we might propagate His message to all of mankind; and may He strengthen us and grant us ease in our affairs and in our struggles in His Path, for He is ever Seeing, and He is the Most Gracious, Most Merciful One, Ameen (*as inspired by the Qur'an, 20:25-28, 33-35, 39-42, 47, 50*).

In the Name of Allah, the Beneficent, the Merciful

57

We ask Allah (SWT) to direct our focus toward the day when the mountains and like-obstacles to the Truth will be scattered as dust and made plain, smooth, and level, with no crookedness or unevenness, and faces shall be humbled and voices lowered in whispers before the Ever Living and Self-sufficient and Beneficent Almighty One, and we will, *Insha'Allah*, follow our beloved Prophet (SAW) and seek his intercession by the permission and pleasure of the Most Gracious and Merciful Lord; and we implore our Creator and Master to guide us and shelter and guard us from evil, and to increase us in knowledge and wisdom, so that we believe and do good works, and we keep up prayers with devoted adhesion, and we praise and glorify Him moment-to-moment, and we engage wholeheartedly in acts of benevolent charity and gracefulness toward all of humankind as well as other creatures; and we ask Him to grant us contentment with what He has apportioned for us in this world so that we do not ever strain our eyes toward the splendor He has provided different classes of people, and that we recognize that this fleeting gift is but a trial, whereas the spiritual sustenance of our Lord and that which our hands send forward to the Hereafter are far better and more abiding, for surely Allah (SWT) is Supremely Exalted, and He is the King of kings, and the Absolute Truth, Ameen (*as inspired by the Qur'an, 20:105-114, 130-132*).

58

May Allah (SWT) purify and sanctify our faith and elevate our level of *Imaan*, and choose us as His slaves who perform acts of goodness toward all of mankind, and may He accept it from us and write it down for us by His Grace and Mercy; and may He unite us all, in love, as a single community – the community of the prophets, the truthful, the martyrs, and the righteous – and we cry unto Him to heed our prayers and to answer our call as He did for his beloved prophets, and to deliver us from all calamities and difficulties and trials and distress and grief that might afflict us; and we plead with Him to never leave us alone but keep us ever close to Him, else we would surely be in a state of utter loss; and may He enable us to follow the illustrious teachings and example of our beloved Prophet (SAW) who was sent as a mercy to all the nations, so that on the day when the heaven is rolled up, much like the rolling up of the scroll of writings, and our Lord rejuvenates creation as He began it at first according to the Promise He has made binding on Himself, we are welcomed in delight with greetings of peace by the angels, and we are spared the grief and tremendous terror of that day, and we are admitted to lofty Gardens of Paradise that rise in magnificence beyond what our souls desire, where we hear not even the faintest sound of the raging Fire of *Jahannam*, but are sublimely content knowing that our Lord is well pleased with us and that this is the day that we were promised, for indeed, our Lord judges with Truth and there is no Gob but He, glory be to Him, the Most High, and He is the Most Gracious and Beneficent, and the Most Merciful of those who show mercy, Ameen (*as inspired by the Qur'an, 21: 76, 83, 87-89, 92, 94, 101-112*).

In the Name of Allah, the Beneficent, the Merciful

59

We ask Allah (SWT), to Whom submit all that is in the heavens and the earth and all of the celestial bodies and all of nature, but, alas, not all of humankind, to make us among those who submit to Him wholeheartedly with body and soul, and to not be like those who have strayed far from the Truth and who call on associates that can neither benefit nor harm them, so that they have lost this world and the Hereafter; or like those who worship Him standing on the verge so that if good befalls them they are satisfied therewith, but if a trial afflicts them, they turn back headlong; and we implore Him to grant us, instead, steadfastness in will and purpose to serve Him in a manner that He truly deserves to be served, and to strengthen our belief and enable us to perform acts of goodness toward all of mankind, so that when we are raised to face Him on the Day of Resurrection, we stand before Him in honor, not abasement, and that He is well pleased with us on that day and admits us to Gardens wherein flow rivers, in peace and joy, by His Grace and Mercy, Ameen (*as inspired by the Qur'an, 22:11-15, 18*).

60

May Allah (SWT) soften our hearts and grant us humility and devotion in submission to Him, and Him alone, so that our hearts tremble when His Name is mentioned; and may He instill in us patience and understanding in facing the trials and afflictions of life; and may He enhance our faith and belief so that we establish prayer along with kind charitable acts of goodness toward all in need, and that we enjoin what is good and forbid evil, and that we perform all these and other acts of devotion that He has appointed for us with clarity of mind and purpose, and with wholehearted enthusiasm and understanding that what ultimately reaches Him is not the physical motions we go through but the true observance of heartfelt duty, for indeed, it is not the eyes that are blind, but blind are the hearts within the breasts; and may He open our hearts to all of humankind and enable us to establish freedom of religion so that we preserve not only mosques, but also cloisters, and churches and synagogues where the Name of Allah (SWT) is much remembered and celebrated, while maintaining our focus on the fact that to Him is the end of all affairs, and that, surely, He is the Strong, the Mighty, the Lord of all the worlds, Ameen (*as inspired by the Qur'an, 22:34-35, 37-38, 40-41,46*).

61

May Allah (SWT) enlighten our minds and open our hearts so that we hold fast to Him and we estimate Him with the sublime estimation that He truly deserves; and that we bow down and prostrate ourselves to Him with devoted prayers in humility and with focused concentration, and we shun and disregard that which is vain and futile, and we purify ourselves by performing acts of charity and goodness for His sake alone, and we keep away from immorality and lewdness, and we faithfully uphold our trusts and covenants, for indeed, such are the successful ones; and we seek His protection and guidance to distance ourselves from those who ascribe partners to Him who, as Allah (SWT) describes, are not only unable to create even a minor creature such as a fly, but are hopelessly unable to even retrieve a speck of food that it might snatch away from them – indeed, weak are both the invoker and the invoked; and we ask Allah (SWT) to direct our paths in the best of manner in both the physical and spiritual worlds and to gift us with a blessed landing in all our travels and affairs as only He can do so; and we implore Allah (SWT) to mindfully turn our faces to Him, the One Who majestically created the heavens and the earth and Who nourishes and sustains them all in due measure, supplemented with rain and gardens of fruit-bearing trees and creatures that provide food and drink for us to enjoy, and Who has made unimaginable means of travel for us, and, most importantly, Who has blessed us with the guidance of Islam, all by His Grace and Mercy, for He is the Strong and Mighty One to Whom all affairs are returned, and He is the Most Excellent Protector and the Most Excellent Helper, Ameen (*as inspired by the Qur'an, 22:73-78, 23:1-22, 23:28-29*).

62

We ask Allah (SWT), the Knower of the seen and the unseen Who is Supremely Exalted above what the ignorant ascribe as partners to Him, and the Lord of the seven heavens and the Lord of the Mighty Throne of Power to Whom belongs whatsoever is in the heavens and in the earth, and in Whose Hand is the kingdom of all things: to protect and guard us against evil and deception, and to keep us ever mindful of Him, for there is no one who can do this but Him; and we beg Him to open the eyes of our hearts so that we fervently believe in His messages and revelations and we constantly live in awe and love of Him, fearful that to Him we must return and account for all our actions and deeds, for such are the ones who hasten to goodness and who are the foremost in attaining them; and we implore Him to keep us united as a single loving community that is devoted in duty toward their Lord and Creator, and to prevent us from fragmenting our hearts and resources and energy into various sects to no avail; and we thank Him profusely for giving us ears and eyes and hearts in both the physical and spiritual worlds, and for multiplying us in the earth and giving us life and a light of guidance to follow, and for granting us His sustenance on earth and promising us a gracious recompense in the Hereafter, for indeed, by His immense Grace and Mercy, He is the Best of Providers in both the worlds, and He is the Most Forgiving, Most Merciful, Ameen (*as inspired by the Qur'an 23:52-53, 57-61, 72, 78-80, 84-92*).

In the Name of Allah, the Beneficent, the Merciful

63

May the Most Exalted Allah (SWT), the Mighty King Who has no partners and is the Lord of the Throne of Grace, grant us refuge from the evil inclinations and suggestions and temptations of the accursed *Shaitaan*, as well as from the *Shaitaan's* misled companions and associates who might try to harm us and who seek to ridicule us, but only to their own loss and detriment while they drift further away from the remembrance of the Almighty Lord; and may He enlighten our hearts and shape our mindset so that we consciously strive to repel evil with that which is best, may it be through a response of goodness that draws people's hearts closer to us, or through some other appropriate means that amends any wrongdoing as per His Will and Purpose; and may He induce patience within us in this struggle and raise and elevate our status and grant us a successful achievement by His Grace and Mercy; and may He forgive us and have mercy on us for, indeed, He is the Most Forgiving and He loves to forgive, and He is the Best of those who show mercy, Ameen (*as inspired by the Qur'an 23:96-98, 109-111, 116-118*).

64

May Allah (SWT), the *Noor-us-Samaawati wal Ardh*, the Light of the Heavens and the Earth, and the Source of all Illumination, grant us refuge in the Light of His Countenance as He did for His beloved Prophet Muhammad (SAW), and may He grant us light in our hearts, light in our *Deen*: our religion, beliefs and way of life, light in our health, light in our advantageous knowledge and wisdom, light in our sustenance, light in our soul, our entire being and in all our affairs, light in our faces, light in our eyes and what we see, light in our ears and what we hear, light in our tongues and what we speak, light in our hands and the work and deeds we do, light in our feet and wherever we go, light in front of us, light behind us, light above us, light below us, light to our right, light to our left, light all around us, light in our flowing water that is blessed by His Grace, Benevolence and Mercy, and ultimately light in our graves along with the immeasurable gift of the highest level of Paradise, *Jannat-ul-Firdaus*, and the coveted sight of His Magnificently Illuminated Countenance, all by His Grace and Mercy, Ameen (*as inspired by the Qur'an, Suratun-Nur [24], and the prayers of the Prophet (SAW)* [3, 4, 5]).

65

We implore Allah (SWT), the resplendent Light of the heavens and the earth that illuminates all of creation in perfection, which no one can diminish no matter how much they struggle to do so, and Whose Light descended on our beloved, illustrious Prophet Muhammad (SAW) so that there was light upon light, and the One Who is in absolute control of all elements of nature and of all blessings, sustenance, and affairs of humankind, and to Whom the entire creation in the universe declares glory, each knowing its prayer and its glorification: to guide us to His Light and to illuminate our mind, body, and soul and to purify us with His Pleasure, and to shelter us from the evil inclinations of the accursed devil, for were it not for His Mercy and Grace, none of us would be pure; and we beg Him to permit His Light to shine in our houses of worship and in our homes, and to exalt these so that His Name is much remembered and glorified therein all day long, devoid of any diversion by the materialistic glitter of the life of this world; and we ask Him to enable us to keep up prayer with due devotion and reverence, and to share the grace He has bestowed upon us with others, and to pardon and overlook the faults of others much like we would like His forgiveness and mercy on the day when the hearts and eyes will turn about in fear of Him; and we seek His protection from the disbelievers, and beseech Him not to make us a trial for them, and to distance us from them, for their deeds are deprived of blessings, much like a thirsty man in the desert who appears to perceive water but, alas, it is only a mirage, and who is engulfed in intense layers of darkness like in the depths of the ocean on a dark day, so that he cannot even see what his own hands are sending forth - indeed, the unfortunate one to whom Allah (SWT) gives not light has no hope for light; and we entreat Him to keep us upright on our feet instead of clinging to the earth, oblivious of the higher values of life, with eyes cast only earthwards, much like His creations that crawl on their bellies or on four limbs; and we fervently invoke His cherished guidance to keep us steadfastly obedient and dutiful and grateful toward Him and to be fearful of Him, and to diligently follow the call of the Prophet (SAW), without undue strong oaths and show of false purity, so that our Lord might make us rulers in the earth and establish us for our religion and grant us security in our affairs, and reward us without measure by His Pleasure, Grace, and Mercy in the Hereafter, gifting us with whatever our hearts desire, along with palaces in gardens wherein flow rivers, a promise well-worth praying for from our Lord and Creator, the Most Gracious, Most Merciful, Ameen (*as inspired by the Qur'an, 24:21-22, 35-46, 51-56, 25: 10, 16, 20*).

66

May Allah (SWT) shine His Light of guidance on us and illuminate our path, and may He induce faith with reverence and remove the darkness of disbelief and evil from all of mankind, much like the rising sun retracts the shadows and leaves brightness in its stead; and may the blessing of His revelations through the Glorious Qur'an dispel ignorance and the drought of knowledge and wisdom, much like the pure water that emanates from the clouds gives life to a dead land and nourishes all living beings; and may He purify our worship of Him and never let us take our low desires as gods besides Him; and may He grant us peace of mind and solace and bliss in our hearts with the sweetness of *Imaan*, and may He establish an inviolable separation between the pathways of our lives and the life of faithlessness and wickedness, much like the barrier that He has created between the river that flows freely alongside the sea, one very sweet and the other salty and bitter; and may He enable us to maintain the ties of blood- and marriage-relationships with pleasure in our hearts and with the coolness of our eyes; and may He constantly assist us in steadfastly striving in His path and in seeking a way to His Pleasure, relying on Him alone, celebrating His praises, and making obeisance to Him with love and devoted obedience, for He is the Most Beneficent and Merciful One, the Ever-Living, established on the Throne of Power, Ameen (*as inspired by the Qur'an, 25: 43-60*).

67

We ask Allah (SWT) to uplift us spiritually into the full resplendence of the Light of His Countenance, so that we walk on earth with dignity and humility, being ever mindful of, and grateful to, the Almighty Lord and Creator; and that we shun falsehood and vanity, and when the ignorant address us we pass by nobly, gently inviting them to the true Peace that exists only in Islam; and that we turn our faces with reverence and full attention towards Him, spending hours of the night in quiet solitude, standing before Him and prostrating to Him, seeking His protection, forgiveness, and mercy, and that we continue this worship through the day, earning an honest living and spending His gift of sustenance in a manner that pleases Him, neither extravagantly nor parsimoniously; and we ask Him to shelter and protect us from ever straying into sinful acts, and to immediately turn us back toward Him in sincere repentance and with goodness when we slip and fall, never being deaf or blind when reminded of His commands and messages, so that He might change our evil deeds into good ones by His immense Kindness; and we beseech Him to grant us in our wives and our offspring peace of mind and the coolness of our eyes, and to make us leaders who guard and advise against evil; and we beg Him to accept our prayers and acts of devotion out of Loving Care for us and to grant us patience, and thereby to admit us to high palaces in the Hereafter, a magnificent abode and resting-place, by His Grace and Mercy, for He is ever Forgiving, Most Merciful, Ameen (*as inspired by the Qur'an, 25:61-77*).

In the Name of Allah, the Beneficent, the Merciful

68

We ask Allah (SWT), the Lord of the worlds Who created us and has shown us the way, to assist and support us and to hold our hand and guide us along the path that is pleasing to Him, for no one else can do so but Him; and we implore Him to assign us friends who encourage us to adhere steadfastly to this righteous path, and we entreat Him to nourish our mind, body, and soul with the best of His sustenance, and to heal us of our ailments of both the body and the soul, and to grant us advantageous knowledge and wisdom, and to ordain for us acts of goodness so that we leave behind a goodly mention in later generations when we depart this world; and we beseech Him to not disgrace us on the day when we are raised again, but to forgive us our mistakes and shortcomings so that we come to Him with a sound heart; and we beg Him to grant us the favorable intercession of our beloved Prophet (SAW), and thereby to make us heirs of the Garden of Bliss along with the righteous and faithful ones, abiding therein with love for our Creator and for all His creations, by His Grace and Mercy, Ameen (*as inspired by the Qur'an, 26:77-104*).

69

We ask Allah (SWT), the Lord of the Mighty Throne Who has no partner whatsoever, to keep us ever mindful of His grace and favors that He has so magnanimously bestowed upon us and on our parents and family; and we beseech Him to enable us to worship Him in sincere submission and thankfulness, and to reflect this gratitude by performing acts of goodness towards all so as to share this gift of favors with others in a manner that pleases Him immensely, such that He thereby admits us into Gardens of Bliss along with His righteous servants by His Grace and Mercy; for indeed, whoever is grateful, is grateful only for his own soul, and whoever is ungrateful, our Lord has no concern for such an unfortunate one, since surely, He is Self-sufficient, Bountiful, and He is Compassionate, Merciful, Ameen (*as inspired by the Qur'an, 27:19, 26, 30, 40*).

70

We ask Allah (SWT) to grant us peace of mind and to nourish us physically and spiritually and to shower His merciful blessings upon us, for He alone sends the winds as good news before His mercy of rain pours from the clouds, and He is the One Who makes beautiful gardens and trees to grow thereby, and has made the earth a pleasant resting-place adorned with rivers and mountains; and we seek His compassion and mercy in uniting us in Truth under the banner of Islam, and we seek His protection in separating us from evil and falsehood, much like He has created a barrier between the fresh, sweet rivers and the salty, bitter seas; and we beg Him to answer our call when we call Him in distress and to remove the harmful evil and ill from us, for He alone is able to do so and to establish us in the earth; and we implore Him for the light of guidance and the sight of wisdom in all walks of life, for He alone can guide us in the darkness of the land and the sea, and He knows the unseen in the heavens and the earth; and we entreat Him with our hands spread out for sustenance for our body and soul from the heavens and the earth, for He alone originates creation and then reproduces it, and He has made everything thoroughly well and has established a mechanism to sustain it all according to a due measure by His will and purpose; and we beseech Him for engraining goodness within us and for granting us security from terror on the day when we are all raised again to stand in His Presence, for indeed, whoever goes aright does so for His own soul, but none can do so without His pleasure and His assistance and support; and we praise Him and thank Him profusely for all His uncountable favors, for surely our Lord is full of grace to men, and He is the All Aware, All Knowing, Ameen (*as inspired by the Qur'an, 27:60-66, 73, 88-93*).

71

We ask Allah (SWT), Who has no partner or associate and to Whom is due all the praise in this life and in the Hereafter, and Whose is the ultimate judgement when everything will perish but Him as we are raised to stand before His Majesty: to grant us protection from any harm we might do to our own souls, and to deliver us from the iniquitous people who might seek to mislead us just as they are misled; and we stand before Him humbly, in dire need for any goodness that He might gracefully bestow upon us; and we beseech Him to grant us the mindset and the ability to persistently seek the blissfully magnificent abode of the Hereafter by means of performing acts of goodness with whatever He has gifted us of His Grace and by refraining from evil and mischief, while not neglecting our portion of the life of this world, being ever thankful for it, but never covetous for it or hankering after it, desiring to exalt ourselves in the earth, for indeed, our Lord amplifies and straitens the means of subsistence for whomsoever He pleases of His servants; and surely, the abode of the Hereafter is to be yearned for, and the reward reserved by Allah (SWT) for those who believe and do good is unsurpassed, and none can receive this except the patiently perseverant ones, all by His Grace and Mercy, Ameen (*as inspired by the Qur'an, 28: 16, 21, 24, 70, 73, 77, 80, 82-83, 88*).

In the Name of Allah, the Beneficent, the Merciful

72

We ask Allah (SWT), the Hearing and Knowing One Who has created the heavens and the earth and has made its elements and cosmic structures of subservient service to us, and Who sustains every living creature according to His apportioned measure in ways that are known and unknown to us, and Who sends down water from the clouds and gives life to a deadened land: to likewise guide us from darkness into light and to enable us to strive hard in His path, worship Him alone in perfect obedience, and perform acts of abundant goodness to all in accordance with this coveted guidance; and we beseech Him to remove our afflictions of the body and heart and soul and to reward us for the very best of our deeds; and we seek the assistance of the Almighty Lord, by His Grace and Mercy, to face any trials He might test us by with grace and nobility and steadfast patience, and to have the love and trust for Him in our hearts so that we never look upon such challenges that are for His sake as His chastisement; and we entreat Him to imbibe in our hearts the love for prayer and to always have His praises on our tongues, for surely prayer keeps one away from indecency and evil and safeguards against the mischief of men, and certainly the remembrance of Allah (SWT) is the greatest and most formidable force, and without doubt, resorting to any other guardian for support besides Allah (SWT) is as frail as seeking shelter in a spider's web; and we implore Him to help us retain focus on achieving the highest level of spiritual advancement, for indeed, the life of this world is but a sport and a pastime, and the home of the Hereafter is the True Life, if only did one really know, Ameen (*as inspired by the Qur'an, 29:2-3, 6-10,30, 41, 45, 60-64, 69*).

73

We ask Allah (SWT), Who originated all creation and then established a mechanism to reproduce it with such awesome ease, and Whose is the exalted state in the heavens and the earth with complete obedience to His Will: to grant us abundant subsistence with favorable winds of benevolence by which we might seek His Grace and taste of His Mercy and Gracious Bounties, and to bless us with rain and flowing water along with spiritual blessings that alight on us by His Pleasure, and to gift us with peace and love and compassion and compatibility and quiet of mind in our spouses, and to join all of mankind in a unified embrace that is blind to the diversity of our varied tongues and colors, for indeed, these are all among His signs for the learned ones who hear and reflect and understand; and we beseech Him to open our hearts towards the near of kin and the needy and the wayfarer with acts of generous charity that reflect His grace upon us, for He is the One Who enlarges provision and straitens it for whomsoever He pleases, and indeed, it is charitable giving, desiring His pleasure, and not usurious dealings, which induces an increase in the property of men and that amplifies blessings manifold; and we entreat Allah (SWT) to set our faces and focus our lives for religion, being upright, and to shape our nature in accordance with the intent by which He created us so that the qualities of pure obedience to Him, dutiful submission to Him, devoted worship of Him in blissful prayer, and the doing of good towards all comes naturally to us without even thinking about it; and we implore Him to keep us united under the guidance of His message in the Qur'an and the sublime teachings and example of His beloved Prophet (SAW), so that we do not split our hearts and our religion into parties, each sect foolishly rejoicing in that which is with it, for there is no altering Allah's creation and there is only one right religion; and we beg Allah (SWT), Who created us in a state of weakness and then gave us strength so that we might fulfil the purpose of our creation by His Grace and Mercy and give thanks thereby, to be merciful towards us and to support us in our old age, whence He might ordain for us by His will and purpose a return to a state of weakness and hoary hair, and we entreat Him to take us unto Himself while life is still good for us, in a state of true belief and goodness of nature, so that He might reward us amply of His grace by His mercy, for He is the Mighty, the Wise, and the Most Forgiving and Merciful One, Ameen (*as inspired by the Qur'an, 30:20-27, 30-32, 37-40, 45-48, 54*).

74

We ask Allah (SWT), the Mighty and Wise One Whose Words and Wisdom are inexhaustible, even if all the trees on earth were used as pens and the seas with seven more like it were used as ink to transcribe them, and the Knowing and Aware One with Whom alone is the knowledge of the Hour and Who alone has comprehensive, intimate knowledge of that which is in the wombs: to gift us graciously from His knowledge and wisdom so that we never foolishly ascribe a partner unto Him, for He, the most High and Great One, is the Truth, and that which the erring ones call on besides Him is simply falsehood; and we beseech Him to guide us so that we are always thankful and grateful to Him as well as to our parents, since indeed, whoever is thankful, is thankful for his own soul, and whoever denies acknowledging the Hand of the Almighty Lord over all affairs is at a loss, for He is the Self-Sufficient, the Praised One Who controls all that is in the heavens and the earth, even if it be the weight of a mustard-seed, or a sapling or water in a rock; and that we take hold of the firmest handle of teachings revealed in the Qur'an and through the traditions of the Prophet (SAW), by keeping up prayer, and enjoining and performing acts of goodness, and forbidding and refraining from acts of wrongdoing, all with patience, for surely, patience is a matter of great resolution; and that we live in humility, never turning our faces away from people in contempt or pride, or going about in the land exultingly, for surely Allah (SWT) loves not any self-conceited boaster; and that we always pursue a right course and speak truthfully in gentle tones, for surely the most hateful of voices is the loud braying of asses; and we entreat Him for blessings and sustenance in all walks of life, for He is the One Who sends down rain from the skies and, indeed, no one knows what he will earn on the morrow or in what land he will die, Ameen (*as inspired by the Qur'an, 31:12-19, 22, 26-27, 30, 34*).

In the Name of Allah, the Beneficent, the Merciful

75

We ask Allah (SWT), Who loves beauty and Who has embellished the heavens and the earth with the most beautiful creations, to beautify our persons and our souls so that we are constantly immersed in celebrating His praises in thankfulness and humility, falling prostrate on our faces when reminded of His glorified messages, and forsaking our beds to spend precious time with Him, calling upon Him in fear and in hope, and graciously sharing and spending the resources He has gifted us with by His immense Grace and Mercy; and we entreat Him to make us among those who submit to Him wholeheartedly in deep belief and understanding, and who are obedient to Him, and are ever truthful, patient, humble, and charitable, and who fast frequently to purify their souls, and who guard their chastity with modesty and honor, and who remember Him much with great awareness moment-to-moment, for such are the ones for whom their Lord has prepared forgiveness with a mighty reward; and we beseech Him to not let us be among the erring ones who have strayed from His path and who need to be chastised so that haply they might turn to Him, but instead, to make us true believers who exercise no alternative choice in any matter when He, *Subhanu wa Ta'ala*, and His beloved Prophet (SAW) have decided an affair and shown a way; and we beg Him to purify and sanctify our actions and accept them from us, and to gift us graciously without measure on the Day of Resurrection, when no soul knows what refreshment of the eyes is hidden from it, an apt reward for what the hands have sent forth, for He is indeed the Most Forgiving, Most Merciful, Ameen (*as inspired by the Qur'an, 32: 7, 15-17, 21, 33:35-36*).

76

We ask Allah (SWT) to make us among the true believers who are forever engrossed in His remembrance with love and devotion, and who glorify Him morning and evening as He deserves, and who keep their duty to Him with dedication and perseverance, and who speak truthful, straight words, and who yearn to remain in the illuminating light of His guidance and who shun the darkness that he has so mercifully brought us out of; and we seek His forgiveness and beseech Him to always put our deeds and affairs in a right state so that we never annoy Him or His messenger or any believer, but love and respect them all with due respect, for indeed, such are the ones who have achieved a mighty success and on whom Allah (SWT) sends blessings and so do His angels; and we call for blessings on our beloved Prophet (SAW), the light-giving sun who has brought us true and perfect guidance from His Lord along with the good news of receiving tremendous grace from the Most Gracious and Merciful Almighty One, and we thank and embrace our loving Prophet (SAW) for illuminating for us the righteous path, and we salute him with a becoming salutation; and we entreat our Creator to make our own salutation on the day that we meet Him to be that of Peace, and to prepare for us an honorable reward and existence in the life of the Hereafter, for surely, our Lord is ever Merciful to the believers, and He is Most Kind and Immensely Gracious, Ameen (*as inspired by the Qur'an, 33:41-47, 56-58, 70-71*).

In the Name of Allah, the Beneficent, the Merciful

77

We ask Allah (SWT), Glory be to Him, Who is the All Truth, and Who obliterates falsehood, which neither originates nor reproduces and prevails, to be our Protecting Friend and Guide and Support, and to be our Loving Companion in the hours of the night that we spend in solitude with Him, worshipping Him and pondering on His Majesty, and in the day when we seek of the bounties that He graciously provides us; and we implore Him to guard us against the machinations of the *Shaitaan*, the Arch-deceiver, and against any wrongdoing or deception in the life of this world, and to always keep us close to Him, and to imprint His revelations on our hearts so that we journey through life in righteousness and without any regrets, for whoever errs does so only to his own loss and no soul can bear another's burden, and whoever goes aright and purifies himself, it is for his own good and due to the mercy of His Lord; and we entreat Him to shape our desires to match His own will and purpose intended for us, so that there is never a barrier between Him and our desires; and we beseech Him to amplify our provision and status, both physically and spiritually, and to keep us ever mindful of His favors upon us, for surely, whatever He grants of His mercy, none can withhold it, and what He withholds, none can grant thereafter, since might belongs wholly to Him, and He is the Wise, the Best of Providers, and is Possessor of power over all things; and we fervently declare our need for our Creator, the Self-Sufficient and Praised One, and beg Him never to remove us from among His favored ones and replace us, but to keep us always aware and enlightened, in His shade, for indeed, the blind and the seeing are not alike, nor are darkness and light, nor the shade and the heat, and neither are the hearing and deaf alike, or the living and the dead; and we implore Him to grant us goodly words and goodly deeds and to exalt our thoughts, words and actions to be worthy of display in His Presence, all by His Grace and Mercy, Ameen (*as inspired by the Qur'an, 34:39, 41, 46-54; 35:1-5, 10, 15-22*).

In the Name of Allah, the Beneficent, the Merciful

78

We ask Allah (SWT), the Magnificent Originator Who has adorned the world with a multitude of creations having a variety of hues and colors, and Who is the Knower of the seen and the unseen in the heavens and the earth, and Who knows intimately what is in the hearts: to imbibe in us an appreciation and understanding of the Noble Book that He has revealed in pure Truth, and to hold us steadfast in our worship of Him and in the doing of good acts, openly and secretly, and we fervently hope that, by His Grace and Mercy, He will grant us thereby His Pleasure along with more gains than we deserve, which perish not, for He is surely the Multiplier of rewards; and we beseech Him to make us among His chosen servants who have inherited the Glorious Qur'an and who are accordingly foremost in performing deeds of goodness, for indeed this is truly a great grace; and we entreat Him to protect us from the proud ones whose evil besets none but themselves and who wait for naught but the unfaltering and definitive course of Allah (SWT) to alight upon them, and to shelter us even from those who reluctantly take a middle course and worship Him merely on the verge; and we fervently seek His love and guidance and grace that will lead to Gardens of perpetuity wherein toil touches us not nor does fatigue afflict us, and where we wear bracelets of gold and silver and our dress therein is silk, and we praise our Creator exuberantly for removing grief from us and for gifting us instead with indescribable Peace, a Word from the Most Merciful Lord, Whose command, when He intends anything, is only to say to it, "Be!" and it is, so glory be to Him in Whose hand is the kingdom of all things and to Whom is our eventual return, Ameen (*as inspired by the Qur'an, 35:28-35, 38, 43; 36:58, 82-83*).

79

We ask Allah (SWT), the Magnificent Creator of the heavens and the earth and the Knower of what's in the hearts, to open our entire being to Islam and to soften our hearts so that we follow the light of guidance and the awesome announcement that He has magnanimously gifted us through the Glorious Qur'an, at which do shudder and tremble those who fear their Lord, and whose skins and hearts then soften in the remembrance of their Lord; and we ask Him to make us among those who listen to the Word of this revelation and understand it and then follow its injunctions in the best of manner, for indeed, only He can grant this guidance, and whomsoever He leaves in error has no guide; and we implore Him to make us ever watchful of our souls, taking care of the Hereafter in obedience and hoping for His mercy, standing and prostrating before Him in solitude in the silent hours of the night; and we entreat Him to make our hearts ever grateful toward Him for He loves this of His servants, and whoever is ungrateful, is indeed misfortunate and Allah (SWT) is above any need; and we beseech Him to ward off from us any evil or harm and to make us among His purified servants who are sheltered and protected by His unmatched Might from the accursed *Shaitaan* who unceasingly seeks to lead us astray, for surely Allah (SWT) is sufficient for His servant, and whomsoever He encompasses in His shade of mercy, none can withhold this coveted mercy from him, and on Him do we rely, as every reliant one must do so, and we hope and pray that when we return to Him and He informs us of what we did, He forgives our shortcomings and purifies us and rewards us for the best of what we did, by His immense Grace and Mercy, for He is the Most Magnificent and Loving Giver, Ever Forgiving and Merciful, Ameen (*as inspired by the Qur'an, 38:35, 82-83; 39:7, 9, 18, 22-23, 35-38*).

80

We ask Allah (SWT) to enable us to keep our duty toward Him, with purity of faith, ascribing no partners unto Him and serving Him alone, and to love Him and be thankful to Him for His immense favors upon us; and we seek His guidance in all our affairs, known and unknown to us, so that we follow His message and directions in the best of manner, and excel in goodness and in the performance of good acts; and we beseech Him to deliver us from evil and from grief and regrets of missed opportunities, and to distance us from the proud and arrogant ones who reject and laugh to scorn at His message and guidance, and who lie against Him, and who will be raised on the Day of Resurrection with blackened, gloomy faces; and we entreat Him to forgive us our shortcomings and to never let us despair of His mercy, for He is indeed the Most Forgiving, Most Merciful; and whenever He takes our souls unto Himself during our sleep, we implore Him to grant us good visions and to join us with righteous souls, and at the ultimate time when He decrees death for us and retains our souls, and the earth beams with the light of its Lord and the Book of Deeds is laid open and the prophets and witnesses are brought up to bear witness and judgement is given, we beg for His forgiveness and His grace and mercy, for surely He is the Most Forgiving, the Most Gracious, and the Most Merciful One, Ameen (*as inspired by the Qur'an, 39:42, 53-61, 65-66, 69*).

81

We wholeheartedly and most gratefully thank Allah (SWT), Who made the earth a resting place for us and the heaven a protective structure, and Who made goodly our forms and provided us with bountiful splendor, and we call on Him, being sincere in obedience to Him, to forgive our shortcomings and sins and to accept our diligent repentance; and we seek refuge in Him from every proud and arrogant one who believes not in the Day of Reckoning; and we implore Him to include us among the true believers for whom the angels who bear the Throne of Power, as well as those around Him who constantly celebrate His praises, pray for protection and shelter from the chastisement of hell; and we entreat Him to heed their supplications to guide us and to guard us against evil, and to admit us into Gardens of perpetuity along with our parents and wives and offspring as are good, for indeed such are the ones who have attained a mighty achievement and on whom the Almighty Lord has showered His immense Grace and Mercy, and surely His Majesty embraces all things in His mercy and knowledge, and He is the Mighty, the Wise, the Ever-living One Who has no partner, the One Who gives life and causes death, and when He decrees an affair, He only says to it, "Be", and it is, so blessed is Allah (SWT) to Whom is our eventual coming, and praise be to Him, the Lord of the worlds, Ameen (*as inspired by the Qur'an, 40:3, 7-9, 27, 64-65, 68*).

82

We call on Allah (SWT) and declare our sincere and obedient submission to Him, and ask Him to make us of the doers of good who repel evil with the best of actions so that even those who have enmity toward us, turn to us with warm friendship, for indeed, none is granted this except the most fortunate, patient ones; and we seek refuge in Him, the All Hearing, All Knowing One, from being afflicted by false imputations from the accursed devil and from even the slightest of pride or arrogance; and we glorify Him night and day, tirelessly; and we beseech Him to guide us and grant us spiritual healing through the Invincible, Glorious Qur'an that He has revealed with Truth, and which He has guarded so that falsehood cannot come at it from before it or behind it, and we beg Him to remove any deafness in our ears or obscurity in our minds in regard to it, and to let it stir our hearts with faith, much like the still earth stirs and swells with life when blessed by rain; and we seek His protection and shelter and ask Him to distance us from those who despair hopelessly when evil touches them, but when the Almighty Lord's mercy lifts their distress, they arrogantly claim that this is due to themselves, for indeed such unfortunate ones will certainly be requited for the worst of what they did; and we entreat Him to make us of those who declare that our Lord is Allah (SWT) and then continue along the right path, so that the angels then descend upon us, giving good news of the promised Garden, in an existence free from fear and grief, and declaring that they are our friends and companions in the life of this world and in the Hereafter, and that we shall have in the afterlife whatever our souls desire and whatever we ask for, an unmatched, welcoming gift from the Most Forgiving, Most Merciful One, Ameen (*as inspired by the Qur'an, 41:27, 30-44, 49-50*).

We ask Allah (SWT), the Hearing and Seeing One, the Originator of the heavens and the earth, and the Absolute One, there being none and nothing like Him: to guide us to the right path through the light of the glorious Qur'an that He has graciously revealed to us, and to grant us inspiration and good visions by His Wisdom to follow this guidance wholeheartedly with intense love for Him; and we beseech the Most Benignant One to gift us with physical and spiritual sustenance from Himself, and to instill in us the proper perspective of desiring the tilth of the Hereafter rather than that of the life of this world, and the understanding that whatever we are given in this life is only a provision for a temporary stay, but that which is with Him in the Hereafter is far better and more lasting, so that we are not deprived in the least of the great grace that He has in store for the ones who believe and do good works; and we entreat Him to shape our character so that we are ever grateful for His countless favors upon us, and that we shun indecency and immorality, and that whenever we are angry we forgive, much as we would like to be forgiven by Him, and that we resort to appropriate consultation in deciding our affairs as directed by Him, and that we keep up prayer and spend meaningfully of whatever resources He has blessed us with, and that we defend mankind against oppression and retaliate against wrongdoing in a proportionate, measured manner, preferring always to amend and forgive with patience, for surely this is a characteristic affair of great resolution, and the reward for such ones is with Allah (SWT); and we plead with Him for protection and security, and we seek refuge against any misfortune that might befall us on account of what our hands have wrought, and we beg Him to pardon and forgive us for our shortcomings, and to heed the prayers of the angels who celebrate the praises of their Lord and ask for forgiveness for those on earth in a manner that the heavens above might almost be rent asunder, for surely besides Allah (SWT) we have no protector nor helper, and He is indeed Forgiving, Merciful, and the Most High, the Great, Ameen (*as inspired by the Qur'an, 42:5, 11, 19- 20, 26, 30-4, 51-52*).

84

We glorify Allah (SWT), the Lord of the heavens and the earth, and the Lord of the Throne of Power, and we submit to Him in thankfulness for having made Himself known to us and for steering us away from the polytheists and from those who ascribe His servants as partners to Him, exalted be His Majesty from what they describe; and we implore Him to guide us by the Glorious Qur'an, which He revealed on a blessed night, and which manifests His Authority and clarifies every affair with wisdom, so that we may lead a life of high value and benefit to mankind, and leave behind us a legacy of goodness that inspires all toward righteousness, unlike those unfortunate ones who leave behind gardens and springs and noble palaces and embellishments at which they rejoiced, but neither the heaven nor the earth wept for them when they departed; and we entreat our Lord to induce us to follow the example and practice of His beloved Prophet Muhammad (SAW), with love and conviction of the heart, and with clarity of sight, unlike the blind ones of yore who foolishly inquired with pride and arrogance as to why the Qur'an was not revealed to a man of importance in their midst, as if they controlled the mercy of their Lord; and we seek His blessings and we bow down and prostrate ourselves out of gratitude to Him for having made all things subservient to us, for indeed, Glory be to Him, we would never have been able to do so ourselves, although sadly, to be sure, man is ever ungrateful; and we implore Him to make us among the God-conscious, dutiful ones, and we beg Him to turn to us with forgiveness and mercy on the day that friends will be foes to one another, except such who keep their duty, for surely, He is Most Forgiving, Most Merciful, Ameen (*as inspired by the Qur'an, 43:13-15, 31-32, 67, 82; 44:3-4, 25-29*).

In the Name of Allah, the Beneficent, the Merciful

85

We praise Allah (SWT), the Mighty, the Wise, the Lord of the heavens and the earth and all the worlds, to Whom belongs greatness in the heavens and the earth, and we ask Him to guide us to the right path and enable us to hold firmly to it, so that there is never any fear or grief that afflicts us due to the displeasure of the Almighty Lord in the life of this world or in the Hereafter; and we turn to Him and humbly submit ourselves to Him and beseech Him to open our hearts in the doing of good to our parents who sacrificed all for our well-being, and to restrain from ever uttering even a sound of disrespect to them; and to make us always thankful for the immense favors He, our Lord and Master, has bestowed upon us; and to induce us to perform acts of goodness that please Him, so that we are among those from whom He accepts the best of their deeds and glosses over their shortcomings and admits them into unimaginable Gardens, a promise of Truth that only He can promise; and we implore Him to distance us from those who transgress and are unjustly proud in the land, and who take their desire as their god and make a jest of the messages of Allah (SWT), and who are blinded by the glitter of the life of this world and who flit away the good things bestowed upon them in frivolous enjoyment, and who conjecture without knowledge that they simply live and die and nothing destroys them but the passage of time, for such are the unfortunate ones whom Allah (SWT) forsakes and leaves in error, covering their sight and sealing their hearing and their hearts, may He protect us from this; and we entreat Him to grant us patience as He did to the messengers, the great men of resolution, so that on the day when the Hour comes to pass and the followers of falsehood perish, and every nation is brought to its knees and is called to account for its actions, and the tenure of time on earth seems like barely an hour, we hope and pray that He will forgive

89

us and have mercy on us and gift us with the sublime pleasure of the sight of His Countenance, for He is the Most Loving One, ever Forgiving and Merciful, Kind and Generous to His servants, Ameen (*as inspired by the Qur'an, 45:22-4, 27-28, 34-37; 46:13, 15-17,19-20, 35*).

86

We ask Allah (SWT) to be our close Patron and to strengthen our belief and *Imaan* and to enhance the flow of guidance to us from Himself as revealed in truth through His beloved Prophet Muhammad (SAW), and to thereby remove any evil within us and improve our overall condition and make firm our feet and grant us the devoted observance of duty; and we seek His assistance and support in facing the trials of life that He has ordained for us so that we might be among those who are steadfast and who strive hard in His way; and we seek His protection from the disbelievers who make mischief in the land, and who cut the ties of kinship, and who follow what the devil embellishes for them while lengthening false hopes for them, for such are the unfortunate ones who are averse to the pleasure of the Almighty Lord and whom He has cursed, and has deafened their ears and blinded their eyes to guidance, and has put locks on their hearts because of their misdeeds, and whose deeds He has rendered fruitless and whose work He has vouchsafed to destroy, their end coming with angels smiting their faces and backs, may Allah (SWT) forbid this from us; and we beseech Him to enlighten our hearts and minds so that we recognize that the life of this world is but a sport and pastime, and to induce us to believe and keep our duty, erase our malice, and be generous with our wealth and resources toward those in need, because whoever is niggardly is so only against his own soul, and Allah (SWT) is Self-Sufficient while we are the needy ones; and we beg Him to let us hold fast to Him and to protect us and preserve our faith, and to never replace us with another people who would be closer to Him, and to admit us into Gardens of Paradise that He has made known to us and that we yearn to receive, by His Grace and Mercy, for He is Most Forgiving, Merciful, and ever Loving and Beneficent toward His servants, Ameen (*as inspired by the Qur'an, 47:1-2, 5-7, 11, 17, 19, 21-28, 31, 36-38*).

87

We glorify Allah (SWT) moment to moment, and pray to Him to bless our beloved Prophet (SAW) who was sent as a mercy to all of creation with the guidance of Truth from the Almighty Lord so that it might prevail over all religions and beliefs, and we ask Him to enable us to aid and revere our honored Messenger, whom we swear allegiance to with the Hand of Allah (SWT) above our hands; and we beseech Him to complete His favor upon us by foremost guiding us to the right path, and we seek His assistance and guidance in being firm against disbelieving tyrants and oppressors but compassionate among ourselves, and to be among those who bow down and prostrate themselves abundantly, yearning for His Grace and Pleasure with their faces revealing their devotion, so that He might be well pleased with us and thereby add faith to our faith, and grant us tranquility in our hearts, and success in both the worlds through all our endeavors; and we entreat Him to cover and forgive our shortcomings and to eradicate any evil within us, and to strengthen our belief and direct us to perform overarching acts of goodness, and to thus lead us into the promised Gardens wherein rivers flow, a grand achievement indeed, all by the Grace and Mercy of the All-Knowing, Wise, and Merciful One, Ameen (*as inspired by the Qur'an, 48:2-5, 9-10, 18, 28-29*).

88

May Allah (SWT) make us true believers and inject faith into our hearts, and grant us nobility in His Divine Presence by enabling us to diligently keep our duty toward Him and to struggle hard in His path with our person and our wealth and lives; and may He inject in our hearts the desire of peace and love for our fellow brethren in faith and, indeed, for all of humankind, recognizing the commonality of our creation and that the purpose of our diversity is to drive us to seek to know each other better; and may He induce in us a noble character so that we do not ridicule others, for perchance they might be better than us, and that we avoid the diseases of the heart pertaining to unsubstantiated suspicion, unjustified spying, and vicious gossiping and backbiting, but instead, we keep our duty to Allah (SWT) so that mercy may be showered upon us; and may He grant us humility in our faith and purity in our hearts so that we never indulge in the audacity of apprising the Almighty Lord of our religion and claiming an obligation by virtue of following Islam, for rather, it is Allah (SWT) Who lays us under an obligation by guiding us to the true faith by His Grace and Mercy, and He knows the unseen of the heavens and the earth and what the mind of man suggests to him, and He is Seer of what we do and is nearer to us than our jugular vein; and when the trumpet is blown on the Day of Judgement and every soul comes with its record to the right and the left, along with a driver and a witness, which respectively impelled him toward evil and called him to the Truth in the life of this world, and hell is asked if it is full and it responds, "Are there any more?", we beseech our Lord to protect and distance us from the threatening hellfire and to separate us from the forbidder of good, the exceeder of limits, the doubter in the Word of His Creator, and to let us instead come to Him with a penitent heart and to admit us with peace into Gardens promised for the one who turns to Him, while upholding the limits and fearing the Beneficent Lord in secret, and to grant us therein all that we desire, and yet more that only He possesses and can provide; and with this fervent hope, we celebrate the praises of our Lord and glorify Him in prostration night and day, and we beg His acceptance and His forgiveness, for He is truly the Most Forgiving, Most Merciful, Ameen (*as inspired by the Qur'an, 49:10-18; 50:16-17, 21, 25, 30-35, 39-40*).

89

We ask Allah (SWT), the Lord of Power and the Irresistibly Strong, the Bestower of sustenance Who gives wealth and contentment, and the One Who makes men laugh and makes them weep, and Who has not created mankind except that they should serve Him: to turn our hearts toward Him so that we flee to Him with dedicated devotion; and we beseech Him to grant us the opportunity and ability to struggle conscientiously in His path, accepting and implementing the Truth revealed to us and then hastening to diligently broadcast and distribute it to others, bearing the load with patience in the process, and being cognizant that man can have nothing but what he strives for and that his striving and its goal are clear to his Creator, Who knows all too well the one who goes aright, and the one who strays from His path while desiring nothing but the life of this world; and we plead with Him to induce patience in us and to always keep us under His Watchful Eyes in all our endeavors; and we entreat Him to enable us to avoid indecencies and immorality, and to be upright and to share our gifts from Him with those who have been denied it, and to perform an abundance of good deeds with goodness, spending the night in worship in quiet solitude and the day in honest work and service of the Lord, but to never ascribe purity to ourselves, for He knows us well ever since we were embryos in the wombs of our mothers; and we pray that we return to our Lord as dutiful servants, with the angels and our beloved Prophet (SAW) interceding favorably on our behalf when we stand before Him on the Day of Judgement, and we sincerely seek His forgiveness and mercy, hoping fervently to be amidst Gardens and fountains on that day, for indeed the Almighty Lord is Most Forgiving, Most Merciful, and immensely Benignant to His servants, Ameen (*as inspired by the Qur'an, 51:1-7, 15-19, 50, 56-58; 52:48; 53:26, 29-32, 39-40, 43,48*).

90

We ask Allah (SWT), the Lord of Glory and Honor Whose Person endures eternally, and the One Who is in a constant state of Glory and is reverently adored by all of nature and all that is in the heavens and the earth, and the Beneficent Lord Who has revealed and taught us the Qur'an and has given us the faculty of expression: to guide us by His Noble Revelation and to enable us to live by it and to spread the Word to others, for indeed He has made the Qur'an easy to remember and understand, if any would but mind and follow it; and we seek His support and assistance and strength in all our endeavors, and we plead with Him to always retain us before His Benevolent and Watchful Eyes, without which we would be utterly lost and overwhelmed and would never be able to overcome our inherent weakness; and we entreat Him to guide and direct us in all our affairs so that we might establish a balance of equity and fairness, never falling short in measure and in our duty in any of our dealings, for indeed, the reward for goodness is but goodness itself; and we prostrate ourselves to the Almighty Lord with thanks for the countless blessings and favors He has bestowed upon us and has ordained for us, both in the life of this world and in what He has in store for us in the Hereafter, Insha'Allah, by His Grace and Mercy, for without doubt, there is no bounty of our Lord that we would deny, and there is nothing that we can offer Him but our dutiful submission, obedience, and gratitude, and there is nothing that we yearn for more than to abide in gardens and rivers in the seat of Truth in the Presence of the Most Powerful King, so blessed be the name of Allah (SWT), the Lord of Glory and Honor, Ameen (*as inspired by the Qur'an, 54:10, 13-14, 17, 54-55; 55:1-4, 6, 9, 27, 29, 60, 77-78*).

91

We ask Allah (SWT), the Incomparably Great Who Is In a constant state of Glory, and the awesome Magnificent One who creates spectacular life from a minuscule seed, and Who provides the blessings of fresh water and vegetation for our sustenance in a manner that we can only observe with awestruck wonder, being utterly unable to do so ourselves, and the One Who has revealed the bounteous, glorious Qur'an for our guidance and has protected its purity for us: to induce this marvelous revelation to penetrate our hearts and to permeate throughout our lives so that we worship Him in pure submission and with deep thanks, immersed in a state of pure peace, as we ought to and by the best of our abilities, although He deserves far more than what we can offer Him; and when the final event that ends existence of life in this world as we know it comes to pass, there being no belying it, and the earth is shaken with a tremendous quaking that crumbles mountains into pieces and scattered dust like carded wool, we beseech Him to exalt us on that momentous day and to avert from us even a modicum of abasement, and we implore Him to include us among the foremost on the right-hand who are drawn nigh to Him and who bask in the Glory of the Countenance of His Face, and to admit us into Gardens of bliss with joy and bounteous delights, where we hear no sinful or vain talk, but only the salutation of Peace, Peace, Peace, all by His immense Grace and Mercy, Ameen (*as inspired by the Qur'an, 56:1-3, 8-14, 25-26, 58-59, 63-65, 68-74, 75-80, 89-91*).

92

We ask Allah (SWT), the Mighty, the Wise, the Possessor of Power over all things, the First and the Last, the Manifest and the Hidden, the Creator and the Magnificent Owner and Sustainer of the universe Who is established on the Throne of Power and to Whom everything in the heaven and the earth declares glory, the One Who is the Seer of all we do and Who is with us wherever we are, knowing intimately well what is in our hearts, and the One Who has revealed the awesome, glorious Qur'an with clarity and with due measure: to enable us to conduct all our affairs righteously in accordance with His sublime message, and to let it penetrate into our hearts and to blot out any darkness within us and to bring us into pure light, much like the rain that gives delightful life to the earth after its death, for surely He is Most Kind and Merciful; and we implore Him to grant us the proper perspective of the life of this world and the wisdom to distinguish between its mere gaiety and vanity, which is only fleeting and will wither away and become chaff like harvested fields, in contrast with the enduring and everlasting Hereafter; and we beseech Him to induce us to vie with one another in the performance of good deeds and in seeking forgiveness, for He is indeed the Lord of Mighty Grace, and to recognize His Will and Purpose that governs the unfolding story of our lives, which is all in a clear book before our Lord brings it into existence, so that we might not grieve at what escapes us, nor exult at what we have been given, for surely Allah (SWT) does not love any arrogant boaster; and we implore Him to save us from niggardliness and the enjoining of it on others, but instead to gracefully offer a goodly portion in the way of the Bountiful Lord Who is the Giver of it all, so that our Almighty Creator may love us for it and grant us an even more generous compensation by His Grace and Mercy; and we entreat Allah (SWT) to make our hearts soft and humble, beating in resonance with His remembrance and that of the Truth which He has revealed, and to enable us to keep our duty towards Him and to follow the example and teachings of His beloved Messenger (SAW), so that on the day when we are raised to stand before Him, we gleam with a brilliant light that envelopes us and that radiates from our right hand by which we are led into Gardens wherein flow rivers, to abide therein for eternity, while those unfortunate ones, who fell into the temptation of the Arch-deceiver and who waited and doubted and indulged in vain and immoral desires, call out to us, begging to borrow from our light, but in vain, for their fate is sealed on that day, may our Lord protect us from this disastrous state and event; and we hope and yearn to receive grace in the life of this world and in the Hereafter from the Lord of Mighty Grace, in Whose Hands alone lies the grace that no one else can control, and to receive light from Him in which we walk, as well as receive forgiveness and mercy, all of which is truly a grand achievement that is manifested at the behest of none other than the Most Forgiving, Most Merciful One, Ameen (*as inspired by the Qur'an, 57:1-6, 9, 11-25, 28-29*).

93

We ask Allah (SWT), the Absolute Beneficent and Merciful Master Who has the most beautiful names and attributes, the King of the universe and the Knower of the unseen and the seen, the Holy, the Author of Peace, the Infuser of Faith, the Granter of Security Who is a Guardian over all, the Mighty, the Wise, the Supreme, the Possessor of Greatness, the Creator, Evolver and Fashioner to Whom everything in the heavens and the earth declares glory in subservience: to enable us to always keep our duty toward Him and to never forget His Majestic Omnipresence, lest He makes us forget the self-preservation of our very souls; and we beseech Him to imbibe deeply within us the revelations, teachings and commands of the Glorious Qur'an, which, if it had been sent down on a mountain, would have crushed and split it asunder out of the fear of the Almighty Lord; and we entreat Him to help us diligently follow the guidance revealed through our beloved Prophet (SAW), and to adopt whatever he enjoined and abstain from whatever he forbade by the Will and Purpose of His Cherished Lord; and we seek the protection and security of our Creator from the accursed devil who misleads treacherously, yet declares himself free of any responsibility out of fear of Allah (SWT), the Lord of the worlds, for surely the disbelievers who follow him are fraught with disunity and weakness; and we implore Him to forgive us as well as our brothers in faith – past, present, and yet to come - and to never let us hold any rancor or spite in our hearts for any of them, and to always keep us united with love for each other and to enable us to offer counsel of goodness and the observance of duty to each other, as well as to abstain from nefariously propagating counsel of sin and disobedience to Allah (SWT) and His Messenger (SAW), for this is the strategy of the devil so that he might cause grief and gain mastery over people and induce them to join his party by making them forget the remembrance of Allah (SWT), may our Lord shelter us from such abasement and the *Shaitaan's* devious machinations; and we beg Him to enlist us instead in His party of believers on whom He has impressed faith and has strengthened with His Holy Spirit from Himself, for indeed, such are the ones who will always prevail, as does the Truth, and such are the ones who are the grand achievers who will inherit Gardens wherein flow rivers, Allah (SWT) being well-pleased with them and they with Him, by His immense Grace and Mercy, Ameen *(as inspired by the Qur'an, 58:9-10, 19-22; 59:7, 10, 13, 14, 16, 18-24).*

In the Name of Allah, the Beneficent, the Merciful

94

May Allah (SWT) guide us to choose our friends and associates meticulously by His Knowledge and Wisdom, so that He is well-pleased with the company we keep and to whom we proffer close relationships, even among our family members following the noble example of Prophet Ibraheem (AS); and may He never make us a trial for arrogant and oppressive disbelievers, but rather filter them out completely from our midst and forgive us our shortcomings and shortsightedness, for He is truly the Mighty, the Wise, ever in a state of Glory in the heavens and the earth; and we beseech Him to clean our hearts of even a modicum of hypocrisy, and to avert from our tongues words of display that we do not adopt into likewise actions, for surely this is most hateful in the sight of our Lord; and may He induce us to strive with all our strength and ability and resources and our lives, while serving in His path in formidable, impenetrable ranks, and to diligently follow the guidance of Islam as revealed to His beloved and honored Messenger (SAW) and be noble helpers in the cause of Allah (SWT), so that we shine with the light of the Almighty Creator and are standard-bearers of His torch, for surely He will perfect His light and make the Truth that He has revealed overcome all forms of falsehood, even though the disbelievers are averse of it and struggle in vain to put it out with their mouths; and may He direct our hearts so that we always turn toward Him and rely on Him, being ever mindful that to Him is our eventual return, and we hope and pray that when we return to Him, He will then, by His Grace and Mercy, forgive us our sins and admit us into magnificent dwellings within Gardens of perpetuity wherein rivers flow, an unparalleled mighty achievement before which all else pales, Ameen (*as inspired by the Qur'an, 60:1, 4-6; 61:1-4, 8-14*).

In the Name of Allah, the Beneficent, the Merciful

95

We ask Allah (SWT), the Mighty, the Wise, the Knower of the unseen and the seen to Whom belongs the Kingdom and the Praise, and Who is in a constant state of Glory in the heavens and the earth, and is the undisputed Possessor of Power over all things: to enable us to hear and obey His call and to keep our duty to Him as best as we can with all our capacity and ability, and to spend generously in His path while we have the breath of life within us, lest we regret not being among the doers of good and then seeking respite when, alas, it's too late, for indeed, Allah (SWT) is the Multiplier of rewards, and whoever is saved from the niggardliness of his soul is truly gifted with success; and we entreat Him to never let our wealth and our family be the cause of our straying from the path of righteousness and truth, for surely these embellishments are but a trial for us and He knows what we conceal within our hearts and what we manifest, and He is the Seer of all that we do; and we thank Him for making goodly our forms and shapes according to His Divine Pleasure, for surely He is Beautiful and He loves beauty; and we beseech Him to likewise beautify our souls and our character, and to never let the glitter of the life of this world distract us from His remembrance, but to enable us to diligently hasten in response to the call for prayers and for performing acts of goodness, and to be thankful to the Almighty Lord as we seek of His Grace, for surely He is the Best of Providers; and we implore Him to protect our hearts from ever being sealed and rendered impervious to His message, as well as to make us shun false and hypocritical speech such as that which emanates from the tongues of clueless, arrogant disbelievers who put on an artificial display, much like objects of wood clad with garments; and we ask Him to soften our hearts and make us among those who pardon and forbear and forgive, just as we will seek His forgiveness on the Day of Gathering, the Day of the Manifestation of Losses, whence we beg Him to purify our souls and purge us of any evil, and to admit us into Gardens wherein rivers flow, to abide therein forever by His Grace and Mercy, for He is Truly the Most Forbearing, and the Most Forgiving, Merciful One, Ameen (*as inspired by the Qur'an, 62:9-11; 63:3-5, 9-10; 64:1-4, 9, 14-18*).

In the Name of Allah, the Beneficent, the Merciful

96

We ask Allah (SWT), the All-encompassing Knower, the Wise, the Absolute Possessor of Power Who knows the measure of all things: to never let us indulge in the slightest in what He has declared unlawful, nor deny or, worse still, make unlawful, that which He has made permissible, but to help us diligently strive in His path and keep our duty toward Him, for surely, whoever does so, the Almighty Lord accordingly makes his affair easy for him and finds a way out of distress for him; and we seek His cherished guidance so that His messages penetrate deep within our hearts and dispel any darkness therein with the light of His Glory; and we entreat Him to make this light gleam ahead of us and to grant us protection as we traverse the journey of this life, and to induce in us the noble characteristics of being His adoring worshippers who are submissive, faithful, and obedient to Him, doers of good deeds and penitent when we slip and stray from His path; and we implore Him to perfect this light for us and to let it radiate brilliantly on our right hand when we stand in judgement before Him, Insha'Allah, as worthy slaves deserving of His Kind Mercy; and we beseech Him to build for us a magnificent mansion in Paradise in His Divine Presence, in Gardens wherein rivers flow, to abide therein forever; indeed, an unmatched, goodly sustenance from the Lord of Grace, Who is the Most Forgiving, Most Merciful, Ameen (*as inspired by the Qur'an, 65:2-4, 11-12; 66:1, 4-5, 8-9, 11-12*).

97

We ask Allah (SWT), the Possessor of power over all things - may He be blessed, in Whose Hand is the Kingdom and Who created the heavens and the earth with no incongruity, and Who gave life and death to test which of us is best in deeds: to guide us so that we walk upright on a straight path, unlike the deprived one who is dragged through life prone on his face, and we implore Him to grant us sublime morals and character as He did for His beloved Prophet (SAW); and we profusely thank him for gifting us with ears and eyes and hearts, and thereby entreat Him that we always listen attentively to His Word, and see with clarity His signs in the universe, and humble and soften our hearts to be worthy of receiving His message and to be filled with His remembrance; and we fear Him in secret, seeking His forgiveness and favor, for surely He is the Knower of subtleties and is uniquely Aware and knows what is in our hearts, whether we conceal it or manifest it; and we beseech Him, the Most Merciful and Beneficent One, for His physical and spiritual sustenance, His protection and security and assistance, and His blessings, for who else is there who can give us sustenance were He to withhold it, or save us from the earth swallowing us up or a violent wind destroying us were He not to grant us security, or help us against His wishes, or bring us flowing water were He to make it subside; and we declare our heartfelt belief in Him and our unswerving reliance on Him, and we prostrate ourselves before His Majesty, and we seek His pardon and forgiveness and mercy, reflecting on the Day of Decision when the unfortunate ones will be called upon to prostrate themselves but will be unable to do so, their looks cast down, abasement covering them, for indeed they were commanded to prostrate themselves while they were yet safe in the life of this world, but refused, may Allah (SWT) forbid this of us, by His Grace and Mercy, Ameen (*as inspired by the Qur'an, 67:1-3, 12-17, 20-23, 28-30; 68:4, 42-43*).

In the Name of Allah, the Beneficent, the Merciful

98

We ask Allah (SWT), the Absolutely Powerful Lord of the east and the west, and the Incomparably Great Who is in a state of constant Glory, to imbibe deep within us the Sure Truth that He has revealed with clear certainty, and to guide us unswervingly thereby, for surely, it is only the retaining ear that will retain this magnificent Reminder; and we seek His forgiveness and mercy whenever we slip and fall short of worshipping Him as He truly deserves, and the same for our parents and the community of believing men and believing women; and we entreat Him to shape our character so that we are among the noble, genuine believers who wholeheartedly accept the revelations of the Almighty Lord and follow His commands diligently, and who are constant at their prayer and guard its sanctity and its due obligations with the highest priority, and in whose wealth there is a known right for the poor and the destitute, and who shun immorality and indecency, and who are faithful to their trusts and covenants, and who are upright in their testimonies, for such are the ones who will receive their accounts in their right hands and be the honored inheritors of lofty Gardens, with pleasant nourishment and fruits near at hand in a life of bliss, a fitting recompense for the deeds sent on before in bygone days, by the Grace and Mercy of the Most Benevolent and Loving Lord, Ameen (*as inspired by the Qur'an, 69:1, 12, 19-24, 51-52; 70:22-35, 40; 71:28*).

99

We ask Allah (SWT) to purify and guide us so that we remember Him much and are constantly aware of His Presence; and that we magnify and glorify Him with complete devotion; and that we arise from our stupor and lead mankind to the path of Truth; and that we shun uncleanliness and likewise clean our hearts to make them worthy of receiving the Word of the Almighty Lord, the Most High; and that we do not proffer any favor seeking gain except for the pleasure of our Lord; and that we are virtuously patient for His sake; and that we keep up prayer and rise secretly in the darkness of the night as best as we can to be with our Creator, for surely this is the firmest way to tread and most effective engagement with our Maker; and that we send forth an abundance of goodness beforehand that is presented to us in joy when we stand before our Majesty; and we beseech Him to hold us steadfast on His path and to enable us to keep at the forefront of our minds the awesome Day of Reckoning, which will make children grey-headed, the day when the guilty ones who are doomed will be asked what brought them into hell and they will respond in regret that they were not of those who prayed, nor did they feed the poor, but they indulged in vain talk and called the Day of Judgement a lie and turned away from the Reminder as if they were frightened asses fleeing from a lion, may Allah (SWT) protect us from this and keep us always mindful of it; and we pledge to be ardently dutiful toward Him and we fervently seek His forgiveness, for indeed, He is Worthy that duty should be kept to Him and He is Worthy to forgive, and He is indeed the Most Forgiving, Merciful, Ameen (*as inspired by the Qur'an, 73:6-8, 17-19, 20; 74:1-7, 42-51, 56*).

100

We thank Allah (SWT) abundantly and we adore Him and glorify His Name morning and evening and throughout long nights, and we plead with Him to guide us so that we hear His Word and see His signs clearly and then let them dwell deep within our hearts and be reflected in our actions, and that we fulfil our vows and tend to the needs of the poor and the orphans and the captive, desiring only Allah's pleasure and expecting neither rewards nor even thanks, but instead, fearing the stern, distressful day, the evil of which is widespread, may Allah (SWT) ward it off from us and grant us refuge and shelter on that day, gifting us with splendor and happiness by His Grace and Mercy, our faces bright, shining with the sight of His Majestic Countenance; and we beseech Him to never replace us but to always keep us steadfast on the path towards Him, for we cannot unless He, the Ever-Knowing, Most Wise Lord, pleases so; and on the day that man stands before Him and is informed of what he sent before and what he put off, we beg for the Almighty Lord's forgiveness and mercy and we entreat Him to purify and bless us with His great kingdom and admit us into magnificent Gardens, reclining on raised couches in perfect comfort with cushions set in rows and carpets spread out, clad in garments of fine green silk and thick brocade and rich bracelets, with fruits near at hand, and a pure drink from the abundantly flowing fountain of *Salsabeel*, wherefrom the servants of the Bounteous Lord drink in crystal and silver goblets tempered with ginger and camphor, exhilarating and purifying to the spirit, all by the immense grace and mercy of the Most Gracious, Most Merciful One, Ameen (*as inspired by the Qur'an, 75:11-13, 22-23; 76:1-22, 25-30, 88:8-16*).

101

We ask Allah (SWT) to make us of those who diligently keep their duty towards Him and who restrain their low desires, fearing to stand before their Lord for judgement, and who accordingly spread goodness far and wide, driving off the chaff, and who are among the foremost to have the distinction of propagating the message of Truth as revealed by the Almighty Lord for regulating all affairs, doing so cheerfully and enthusiastically, with passionate vehemence; and we implore Him to enable us to maintain a sharp focus on the overwhelming event of the Day of Decision, when the angels will stand in ranks and none shall speak except the one that the Beneficent Master permits, and he shall speak aright, and man will sense that he tarried on earth for but an evening or a morning, and the rejecters of the Truth and the proponents of falsehood will see what their hands have sent forth and will be full of woe, with faces downcast, laboring, toiling, and lamenting that perchance they might have taken a way to their Lord and wishing that they were mere dust; and on that momentous Day of Truth when such disbelievers will be given to eat food of just thorns and to drink only boiling or intensely cold water, a fitting requital for their extreme actions, we beg our Lord to grant us refuge in Himself, and to illuminate our faces with the Radiant light of His Countenance, smiling and laughing in exhilarating happiness, joyous for having striven in His path, and to admit us into lofty Gardens of bliss, in delight and loving care, for He is indeed the Most Affectionate One, Ever Forgiving, and Most Merciful, Ameen (*as inspired by the Qur'an, 77:1-6, 13-15; 78:24-26, 38-40; 79:1-5, 40-46; 80:38-39; 88:1-10*).

In the Name of Allah, the Beneficent, the Merciful

102

We ask Allah (SWT), the Lord of the worlds, to hold our hands and guide us along the straight path as perfected by Him in the final Reminder revealed for all the nations, because indeed, we can only go aright if He so pleases; and we entreat Him to enable us to be faithful, in love and obedience, towards His beloved, bountiful Messenger, who is established in the presence of the Lord of the Throne; and we beseech Him to maintain in the forefront of our minds the day when we shall stand before Him in judgement, and to accordingly sanctify and purify all our affairs, known and unknown to us, so that we deal with fairness and equity and honesty toward all, just as we expect the full measure of our own dues; and on that day when the command is solely Allah (SWT)'s and no soul will control aught for another soul, we beg Him to forgive us and, by His mercy, thoroughly cleanse our book of deeds so that it is recorded in the highest of places, and to let us be drawn near to His Majesty to witness it, and to let us be given to drink from a fountain tempered with water that is sealed with musk, coming from above by His Grace, and to admit us into Gardens of Delight with our faces brightened by bliss, reclining in absolute peace on raised couches with cushions on hand, and we implore Him to let this be what we aspire and strive to attain throughout our lives, looking forward most of all to the bounteous sight of the Glorious Countenance of the Almighty Lord, the Most Beneficent, Most Merciful, Ameen (*as inspired by the Qur'an, 81:19-21, 27-29; 82:17-19; 83: 1-6, 18-28*).

103

We ask Allah (SWT), the Most High and Glorious One, Doer of what He intends, Who creates and fashions unto perfect form, then accords a measure as per His Divine Will and Purpose and provides guidance: to complete this favor upon us by imbibing within our hearts and cultivating in our actions the injunctions and teachings of the Glorious Qur'an, the awe-inspiring revelation that He has preserved in a guarded tablet, and to make us among those who remind mankind with wisdom and gentle reasoning, and who adore Him immensely for having revealed this treasure to us, may it profit us all; and we beseech Him to shape our mindset and lives so that we are in a state of constant remembrance of Him, and that we purify ourselves and worship Him devotedly and perform acts of overarching goodness, realizing that it is not the life of this world that we must prefer and be consumed by, but it is the Hereafter that should be our focal point, since this is better and more lasting; and we entreat Him to grant us the aptitude and patience to strive hard in His path until the time we meet Him, so that we do so with honor and, by His Grace and Mercy, attain the grand achievement of inheriting Gardens wherein rivers flow, for indeed, such are the ones who are successful, and surely, He is the Most Forgiving, Loving, Lord of the Throne of Power, Ameen (*as inspired by the Qur'an, 84:6, 21; 85:11, 14-16, 21-22; 87:1-3, 9-10, 14-17*).

104

We ask Allah (SWT), Who is the Master of the life of this world and the Hereafter, and to Whom belongs the dominion for showing humankind the way: to guide us and facilitate our tasks so that we strive in His path with ease, and keep our duty toward Him with due diligence, and spread goodness all around us with grace; and we beseech Him to strengthen our resolve so that we adopt the uphill road with clarity of vision, speech and actions, which is the road of the people of the right hand who believe and exhort one another to the Truth and to patience and goodness and acts of mercy, and who struggle against tyranny and oppression in order to achieve freedom for all of mankind, and who feed the needy ones in days of hunger, and who lift and offer relief to the poor lying in the dust, and who honor the orphans, and who shun the devouring of rightful heritage and the excessive love of wealth, and we fervently seek His support and assistance in this noble endeavor, for surely, man is created to face difficulties; and we entreat Him to open our hearts so that we share the resources He has so graciously gifted us with those in need, seeking not even a word of thanks or any boon for a reward except the pleasure of the Lord, the Most High, and the sight of His Magnificent Countenance, for surely such are the successful ones who are pleasing to their Creator and who cause their souls to grow to perfection and will themselves be well-pleased; and we seek His shelter and protection from being of those who bury their souls in the dust, and who will regret in despair and distress in the Hereafter in a state of loss, lamenting that if only they had sent before something of goodness for this afterlife; but instead, we hope and pray that our souls are at sublimely peaceful rest on that day, returning to their Lord well-pleased and well-pleasing, entering Gardens of bliss along with the Almighty Lord's honored servants, by His Grace and Mercy, Ameen (*as inspired by the Qur'an, 89:17-20, 24, 27-30; 90:4-18; 91:7-10; 92:4-7, 12-13, 17-21; 95:6; 103:2-3*).

In the Name of Allah, the Beneficent, the Merciful

105

We profusely thank Allah (SWT) for guiding us whenever He finds us groping in the dark, and for enriching us physically and spiritually whenever He finds us in want, and for expanding our breasts and illuminating us with wisdom, and for teaching us by the pen and His enlightened Words that which we know not, and for providing us with shelter and security and refuge from all sorts of ills and dangers, and for removing from us the burden that weighs down our backs, and for exalting our mention in this life and in the Hereafter; and we beseech Him to enable us to proclaim His immense countless favors upon us by worshipping Him alone and making Him the exclusive desire to please in all respects, as well as by striving hard in His path and dealing with kindness and attentiveness to the orphans and the oppressed and the neglected ones and those in need; and we entreat Him to grant us ease from difficulties along with the understanding that the state of the soul in the Hereafter is far more important than the life of this world; and we beg Him to never forsake us or be displeased with us, but to love us and to amplify our acts of devotion and worship and to multiply its virtues manifold, much as He has promised to do for worshipping Him during *Lailat-ul-Qadr*, the Night of Power and Decree, and we ask Him to graciously perpetuate such blessings throughout our lives, so that the angels and the Spirit descend upon us by His permission and aid and bless us in all our affairs; and we implore Him to gift us with the majestic state of peace with which we are well-pleased, and particularly so with the ultimate, incomparable and unfathomable level of Peace when we eventually return to Him for eternity, by His Grace and Mercy (*as inspired by the Qur'an, 93:3-11; 94:1-8; 96:3-5; 97:3-5*).

106

We ask Allah (SWT) to grant us the cherished gift of guidance in following the right religion as propounded in the pure pages of the Glorious Qur'an revealed to His beloved Prophet (SAW), which encompasses all previous revelations, and to inspire our hearts to serve Him alone, being sincere in obedience to Him and fearful of His displeasure, and to be upright, with enlightened prayers and with heartfelt service to Muslims and mankind at large by virtue of our wealth, words, cheerfulness, and actions, so that we truly earn the coveted title of being the best of His creatures; and we implore Him to imbibe within our hearts sincere gratitude for this immeasurable favor, and to let it be reflected in our character and actions, for surely man is ungrateful to His Lord and niggardly on account of the love of wealth, to which he bears witness against himself; and when the earth is shaken with her final awesome trembling, and the mountains disintegrate like carded wool, and men are scattered like moths as they arise from their graves, and that which is in the breasts becomes manifest, and whoever has done an atom's worth of goodness or evil sees it then with clarity of sight, while their Lord makes them transparently aware of it, we beg our Almighty Creator for forgiveness and mercy, and beseech Him to let the measure of our good deeds be heavy so that we earn His Pleasure and are thereby admitted to the highest level of Gardens of perpetuity wherein rivers flow, to lead a most pleasant afterlife, a blessing that is reserved for those with whom Allah (SWT) is well-pleased, and for which they are well-pleased with Him, Ameen (*as inspired by the Qur'an 98:2-3, 5, 7-8; 99:1, 7-8; 100:6-11; 101:4-7*).

107

We ask Allah (SWT), the Self-subsisting One Who has no partner and is the Incomparably Great, to bless us with an abundance of goodness in this life and in the Hereafter, most of all being the sight of His Majestic Countenance and the tryst at the pool of *Kauthar* with our beloved Prophet (SAW) and his noble companions, and may He enable us to attain this immense blessing by dedicating our lives to worshiping Him devotedly and exclusively, celebrating His praises through our thoughts, words and actions, and through selfless sacrifice of our time, energy, and wealth for the elevation of the condition of Muslims and the betterment of mankind to the best of our ability, all done for His sake alone; and we entreat Him to grant us protection and security and to cut off the roots of those who intend to harm us; and we beseech Him to increase our *Imaan* and to preserve our heart and soul from any loss of benefits that He has reserved for those whom He has blessed, and to enlist us among those who invite mankind to the beautiful and sacred Truth that He has revealed through His beloved Prophet (SAW), and may He grant us *Sabr* in our acts of worship and obedience to Him, our trials, our attitudes in life, and in all our dealings and relationships, and may He direct us to likewise exhort one another to patience, and to be among those who strive to uplift the orphans and support the ones in need and distress, unlike those who belie religion and perform acts of worship only to be seen of men while refraining from even small acts of kindness, nor like those who slander and defame and who amass wealth as if it will make them abide forever, all the while being blindly diverted by abundance in this life until such time as they come to the graves, may Allah (SWT) protect us from such an existence; and we thank the Almighty Lord Who feeds us, physically and spiritually, and Who gives us security from fear; and we implore Him to choose us and assist us to serve Him, so that when His victory is manifested and we see mankind turning towards Him in obedience *en masse*, He might count us among His slaves and servants who strove in His path with the intention to achieve this end; and on the day when all of mankind will see the Truth with certainty of sight, which they should have inferred and realized by virtue of the abundant signs the Magnificent Creator has revealed in this world, we beg Him to forgive us and have mercy on us and to admit us by His Pleasure to the most pleasurable and delightful Gardens wherein rivers flow, by His Grace and Mercy, for He is the Most Forgiving, Most Merciful, Ameen (*as inspired by the Qur'an, 102:1-2, 7-8; 103:1-3; 104:1-3; 106:3-4; 107:1-7; 108:1-3; 110:1-3; 112:1-4*).

108

We seek refuge in Allah (SWT), the King of kings, Who is the Lord and Master of all creations, and we seek His guidance and inspiration and blessings so that our love and consciousness of Him permeates through our entire being and illuminates our faces and hearts like the rising sun at dawn, and we ask His Divine Majesty, the Lord of Dawn, to prevent the *Shaitaan* from casting his shadow to diminish our illumination; and may Allah (SWT) grant us of His Grace so that our affairs are never enveloped in darkness, and may He shelter us with His impenetrable shield and protection so that the whisperings and evil suggestions and spells of the *Shaitaan* are dispelled and remain ever remote from us, and may He grant us success thereby as well as deflect from us the envy of those who are envious because of the grace and mercy that He, Allah (SWT), has most graciously bestowed upon us; and we entreat Him to protect us and grant us safety and security from the evil whisperings and temptations and false promises of *Shaitaan*, who instigates and whispers evil into the hearts of men and then slinks away after ensnaring them, declaring that he is clear of them, may Allah (SWT) forbid, and may He forgive us and have mercy on us, for He is truly the Most Forgiving, Most Merciful, Most Forbearing, Ameen (*as inspired by the Qur'an: 113:1-5; 114:1-6, 8:48*).

109

As taught by Allah (SWT) in His divine revelations through the Qur'an and through the teachings of the Prophet (SAW), we ask for protection and refuge in the Almighty Lord and *Rabb* (the Creator, Nourisher, Sustainer) against fear, grief, and anxiety, and from lack of strength and courage, and from laziness and inaction, and from miserliness and smallness of the heart, and from the burden of debt, and from the devastation of the soul through pride and arrogance, and from the debilitation of ill-health and the decrepitude of old age, and from dependence on anyone except Him alone, and from all forms of harm and evil, and we implore Him for *Taqwa* (God-consciousness and nearness to Him) and the purification of our souls, and for solace and tranquility of the heart, and for all the goodness that His beloved Prophet (SAW) asked Him for in regard to this world and the Hereafter, which we fervently hope to receive by His Grace and Mercy, Ameen.

110

The following concluding Du'aa is called Du'aa-e-Qunoot" [6], and is fittingly recited (in Arabic) in the final Rakaah of Salah during the *Witr* prayer each day, and is a beautiful all-encompassing invocation:

"Oh Allah (SWT), we invoke Thee for help and beg Thee for forgiveness, and we believe in Thee and put our trust in Thee, and we praise Thee in the best way, and we thank Thee and we are not ungrateful to Thee; and we forsake and turn away from the one who disobeys Thee; Oh Allah (SWT), we worship Thee and pray to Thee and prostrate ourselves before Thee; and we hasten towards Thee and serve Thee; and we hope to receive Thy mercy, and we dread Thy torment; surely, the rejecters of faith shall incur Thy torment," Ameen.

References

1. "The Holy Qur'an", English translation of meaning and commentary by Maulana Muhammad Ali, seventh edition, 1991.

2. "The Holy Qur'an", English translation of meaning and commentary by Maulana Yusuf Ali, third edition, The Islamic Center, Washington, D.C., 1938.

3. "Sahih al-Bukhari", English translation of meaning by Muhammad Muhsin Khan, Vols 1-9, Kazi Publications, Lahore, Pakistan, fourth edition, 1976.

4. "Sahih Muslim", English translation of meaning by Abdul Hamid Siddiqi, Vols 1-4, Kitab Bhavan, New Delhi, 1977.

5. "Sunan Abu Dawud", English translation of meaning by Ahmad Hasan, Vols 1-2, Muhammad Ashraf Publishers, Lahore, 1984.

6. "Everyday Fiqh," Vols 1-2, Mohammad Yusuf Islahi, English translation of meaning by Abdul Aziz Kamal, revised by Muzzammil H. Siddiqui, Maktaba Zikra, Delhi, India, 1990.

7. "Fiqh us-Sunnah," Vols 1-5, English translation of meaning by Muhammad Sa'eed Dabas and Jamal al-Din M. Zarabozo, American Trust Publications, 1989.

Glossary of Terms

SWT: *Subhanu wa Ta'Aala*: Glory be to Him (God), the Most High.

SAW: *Sallallahu Alaihe wa Sallam*: Peace and blessing be upon him.

AS: *Alaihis-Salaam*: Peace be on him.

RA: *Radhi Allahu Anhu/Anha*: May Allah be pleased with him/her.

Aayat: Verse from the Qur'an; also Word or Sign conveying value, purpose and significance from Allah (SWT).

Adhan: Principal call for ritual prayers.

Alhamdulillah: Praise (and thanks) be to Allah (SWT).

Allahu Akbar: Allah (SWT) is great.

Ameen: May Allah (SWT) accept (as in "Amen").

Barakah: Flow of blessings and grace from Allah (SWT) with respect to all physical and spiritual aspects.

Deen: Way of life as a religion.

Dhikr: Remembrance of Allah (SWT), typically through repeated recitation of His attributes and through invocations and supplications.

Du'aa: Invocation (or supplication) made to Allah (SWT).

Ebraheem: Abraham, peace be on him.

Fiqh: Jurisprudence in Islam.

Hadith: Narrations of traditions of the Prophet (SAW), containing his sayings and accounts of his practices (*sunnah*), as well as some of those of his companions (*Ahadith*: plural form of *Hadith*).

Hadith-ul-Qudsi: Sacred narration from Allah (SWT), but related by the Prophet (SAW).

Hajj: Pilgrimage to Makkah, required of all Muslims once in a lifetime, given adequate health and affordability.

Halaal: Permissible by Islamic law.

Haram: Sinful or forbidden by Islamic jurisprudence.

Hijrah: Migration, typically referring to the migration of Muslims (including Prophet Muhammad (SAW)) from Makkah to Madinah (in June/July 622 CE).

Ibadat/Ibadah: Act of worship, entailing obedience, submission, and devotion to Allah (SWT).

Iblis: Devil (or *Shaitan*), who was of the creation called the Jinn (made of fire), and who refused to bow to Adam (AS) when commanded by Allah (SWT) to do so.

Imaam: Leader in prayers.

Imaan: Faith, including belief in Allah (SWT), His angels, His prophets, His Divine books (including the Psalms of David, the revelation to Abraham, the Gospel, the Torah, and the Qur'an), the Day of Judgment, and destiny (Divine decree).

Insha'Allah: If Allah (SWT) wills.

Jahannam: Hell.

Jannat: Heaven or Paradise.

Jumu'ah: Friday (auspicious day for Muslims, including a day for a special compulsory congregational prayer).

MashaAllah: It pleased Allah (SWT).

Masjid: Formally established place of worship for Muslims, which is designated as a house of Allah (SWT).

Mehraj: Spiritual night journey undertaken by Prophet Muhammad (SAW) from Masjid-al-Aqsa in Jerusalem to the heavens to converse with Allah (SWT) (also the occasion during which the five ritual prayers for Muslims were ordained).

Muslim: One who has submitted in faith to Allah (SWT) and has accepted Prophet Muhammad as His final messenger.

Mu'min: A practicing Muslim whose heart is firmly established in the faith of Islam.

Musallah: A place of prayer that has not been formally sanctified as a Masjid or is a temporary place of prayer (sometimes also referring to a prayer mat).

Nafs: Soul or self or ego.

Rakah: Single unit or cycle of the Islamic ritualistic prayer.

Ramadan: Ninth month of the Islamic lunar calendar during which Muslims are required to observe a fast (in a prescribed manner, both physically and morally) from dawn until sunset.

Rasool Allah: Messenger of Allah (SWT), typically referring to Prophet Muhammad (SAW) himself in an alternative form.

Sabr: Patience, perseverance, forbearance, restraint, tolerance, resolve.

Sadaqah: Charity.

Sahaba: Companions of the Prophet (SAW). (In singular form: *Sahabi* for males and *Sahabiyah* for females).

Sajdah: Prostration to Allah (SWT) (as typically performed in ritual prayers).

Salaat (*Salaah*): Ritual prayers for Muslims, including the *Fajr* (dawn), *Zuhr* (afternoon), *Asr* (late afternoon or evening), *Maghrib* (sunset), and *Isha* (night) prayers.

Sawm: Fasting.

Shaitan: Devil (see Iblis).

SubhanAllah: Glory be to Allah (SWT).

Sujood: see *sajdah*.

Sunnah: Practice (way of life or path) of the Prophet (SAW), including his teachings and sayings.

Surah: Chapter, referring typically to a chapter of the Qur'an.

Tahajjud: Voluntary night prayer, which is strongly encouraged in order to draw closer to Allah (SWT).

Taqwa: God-consciousness, mindfulness, and piety, and in general, to avoid what displeases Allah (SWT) and to enjoin what pleases Him.

Qayamat: Day of Judgment.

Qur'an: The Divine book revealed from Allah (SWT) in His own Words to Prophet Muhammad (SAW); literally, *"The Recitation"*.

Ummah: Community or nation, referring typically to the Muslims.

Wahy: Direct revelation from Allah (SWT), as for example the revelation of the verses of the Qur'an.

Zakaat (Zakaah): Mandatory prescribed annual charity (2.5% of wealth (other than daily-use assets such as personal dwelling), which is in possession over the year, given that it exceeds a prescribed minimum).

Printed in the United States
By Bookmasters